THE
FINER GRAIN

HENRY JAMES

The Finer Grain

Henry James

© 1st World Library, 2007
PO Box 2211
Fairfield, IA 52556
www.1stworldlibrary.com
First Edition

LCCN: 2007934123

Softcover ISBN: 978-1-4218-9648-9
Hardcover ISBN: 978-1-4218-9748-6
eBook ISBN: 978-1-4218-9548-2

Purchase *"The Finer Grain"*
as a traditional bound book at:
www.1stWorldLibrary.com/purchase.asp?ISBN=978-1-4218-9648-9

1st World Library is a literary, educational organization
dedicated to:

- Creating a free internet library of downloadable ebooks

- Hosting writing competitions and offering book publishing
scholarships.

Interested in more 1st World Library books? contact:
literacy@1stworldlibrary.com
Check us out at: www.1stworldlibrary.com

1st World Library Literary Society

Giving Back to the World

"If you want to work on the core problem, it's early school literacy."

- James Barksdale, former CEO of Netscape

"No skill is more crucial to the future of a child, or to a democratic and prosperous society, than literacy."

- Los Angeles Times

"Literacy... means far more than learning how to read and write... The aim is to transmit... knowledge and promote social participation."

- UNESCO

"Literacy is not a luxury, it is a right and a responsibility. If our world is to meet the challenges of the twenty-first century we must harness the energy and creativity of all our citizens."

- President Bill Clinton

"Parents should be encouraged to read to their children, and teachers should be equipped with all available techniques for teaching literacy, so the varying needs and capacities of individual kids can be taken into account."

- Hugh Mackay

CONTENTS

"THE VELVET GLOVE"

I

HE thought he had already, poor John Berridge, tasted in their fulness the sweets of success; but nothing yet had been more charming to him than when the young Lord, as he irresistibly and, for greater certitude, quite correctly figured him, fairly sought out, in Paris, the new literary star that had begun to hang, with a fresh red light, over the vast, even though rather confused, Anglo-Saxon horizon; positively approaching that celebrity with a shy and artless appeal. The young Lord invoked on this occasion the celebrity's prized judgment of a special literary case; and Berridge could take the whole manner of it for one of the "quaintest" little acts displayed to his amused eyes, up to now, on the stage of European society—albeit these eyes were quite aware, in general, of missing everywhere no more of the human scene than possible, and of having of late been particularly awake to the large extensions of it spread before him (since so he could but fondly read his fate) under the omen of his prodigious "hit." It was because of his hit that he was having rare opportunities—of which he was so honestly and humbly proposing, as he would have said, to make the most: it was because every one in the world (so far had the thing gone) was reading "The Heart of Gold" as just a slightly too fat volume, or sitting out the same as just a fifth-act too long play, that he found himself floated on a tide he would scarce have dared to show his favourite hero sustained by, found a hundred agreeable and interesting things happen to him which were all, one way or another, affluents of the golden stream.

The great renewed resonance—renewed by the incredible luck of the play—was always in his ears without so much as a conscious turn of his head to listen; so that the queer world of his fame was not the mere usual field of the Anglo-Saxon boom, but positively the bottom of the whole theatric sea, unplumbed source of the wave that had borne him in the course of a year or two over German, French, Italian, Russian, Scandinavian foot-lights. Paris itself really appeared for the hour the centre of his cyclone, with reports and "returns," to say nothing of agents and emissaries, converging from the minor capitals; though his impatience was scarce the less keen to get back to London, where his work had had no such critical excoriation to survive, no such lesson of anguish to learn, as it had received at the hand of supreme authority, of that French authority which was in such a matter the only one to be artistically reckoned with. If his spirit indeed had had to reckon with it his fourth act practically hadn't: it continued to make him blush every night for the public more even than the inimitable *feuilleton* had made him blush for himself.

This had figured, however, after all, the one bad drop in his cup; so that, for the rest, his high-water mark might well have been, that evening at Gloriani's studio, the approach of his odd and charming applicant, vaguely introduced at the latter's very own request by their hostess, who, with an honest, helpless, genial gesture, washed her fat begemmed hands of the name and identity of either, but left the fresh, fair, ever so habitually assured, yet ever so easily awkward

Englishman with his plea to put forth. There was that in this pleasant personage which could still make Berridge wonder what conception of profit from him might have, all incalculably, taken form in such a head—these being truly the last intrenchments of our hero's modesty. He wondered, the splendid young man, he wondered awfully, he wondered (it was unmistakable) quite nervously, he wondered, to John's ardent and acute imagination, quite beautifully, if the author of "The Heart of Gold" would mind just looking at a book by a friend of his, a great friend, which he himself believed rather clever, and had in fact found very charming, but as to which—if it really wouldn't bore Mr. Berridge—he should so like the verdict of some one who knew. His friend was awfully ambitious, and he thought there was something in it—with all of which might he send the book to any address?

Berridge thought of many things while the young Lord thus charged upon him, and it was odd that no one of them was any question of the possible worth of the offered achievement—which, for that matter, was certain to be of the quality of *all* the books, to say nothing of the plays, and the projects for plays, with which, for some time past, he had seen his daily post-bag distended. He had made out, on looking at these things, no difference at all from one to the other. Here, however, was something more—something that made his fellow-guest's overture *independently* interesting and, as he might imagine, important. He smiled, he was friendly and vague; said "A work of fiction, I suppose?" and that he didn't pretend ever to pronounce, that he in fact quite hated, always, to have to, not "knowing," as he felt, any better than any one else; but would gladly look at anything, under that demur, if it would give any pleasure. Perhaps the very brightest and most diamond-like twinkle he had yet seen the star of his renown emit was just the light brought into his young Lord's eyes by this so easy consent to oblige. It was easy because the presence before him was from moment to moment, referring itself back to some recent observation or memory; something caught somewhere, within a few weeks or months, as he had moved about, and that seemed to flutter forth at this stir of the folded leaves of his recent experience very much as a gathered, faded flower, placed there for "pressing," might drop from between the pages of a volume opened at hazard.

He had seen him before, this splendid and sympathetic person—whose flattering appeal was by no means *all* that made him sympathetic; he had met him, had noted, had wondered about him, had in fact imaginatively, intellectually, so to speak, quite yearned over him, in some conjunction lately, though ever so fleet-ingly, apprehended: which circumstance constituted precisely an association as tormenting, for the few minutes, as it was vague, and set him to sounding, intensely and vainly, the face that itself figured everything agreeable except recognition. He couldn't remember, and the young man didn't; distinctly, yes, they had been in presence, during the previous winter, by some chance of travel, through Sicily, through Italy, through the south of France, but his *Seigneurie*—so Berridge liked exotically to phrase it—had then (in ignorance of the present reasons) not noticed *him*. It was positive for the man of established identity, all the while too, and through the perfect lucidity of his sense of achievement in an air "conducting" nothing but the loudest bang, that this was fundamentally much less remarkable than the fact of his being made up to in such a quarter now. That was the disservice, in a manner, of one's having so much imagination: the mysterious values of other types kept looming larger before you than the doubtless often higher but comparatively familiar ones of your own, and if you had anything of the artist's real feeling for life the attraction and amusement of possibilities so projected were worth more to you, in nineteen moods out of twenty, than the sufficiency, the serenity, the felicity, whatever it might be, of your stale personal certitudes. You were intellectually, you were "artistically" rather abject, in fine, if your curiosity (in the grand sense of the term) wasn't worth more to you than your dignity. What was your dignity, "anyway," but just the consistency of your curiosity, and what moments were ever so ignoble for you as, under the blighting breath of the false gods, stupid conventions, traditions, examples, your lapses from that consistency? His *Seigneurie*, at all events, delightfully, hadn't the least real idea of what any John Berridge was talking about, and the latter felt that if he had been less beautifully witless, and thereby less true to his right figure, it might scarce have been forgiven him.

His right figure was that of life in irreflective joy and at the highest thinkable level of prepared security and unconscious insolence. What was the pale page of fiction compared with the intimately personal adventure that, in almost any direction, he would have been all so stupidly, all so gallantly, all so instinctively and, by every presumption, so prevailingly ready for? Berridge would have given six months' "royalties" for even an hour of his looser dormant consciousness—since one was oneself, after all, no worm, but an heir of all the ages too—and yet without being able to supply chapter and verse for the felt, the huge difference. His *Seigneurie* was tall and straight, but so, thank goodness, was the author of "The Heart of Gold," who had no such vulgar "mug" either; and there was no intrinsic inferiority in being a bit inordinately, and so it might have seemed a bit strikingly, black-browed instead of being fair as the morning. Again while his new friend delivered himself our own tried in vain to place him; he indulged in plenty of pleasant, if rather restlessly headlong sound, the confessed incoherence of a happy mortal who had always many things "on," and who, while waiting at any moment for connections and consummations, had fallen into the way of talking, as they said, all artlessly, and a trifle more betrayingly, against time. He would always be having appointments, and somehow of a high "romantic" order, to keep, and the imperfect punc-tualities of others to wait for—though who would be of a quality to make such a pampered personage wait very much our young analyst could only enjoy asking himself. There were women who might be of a quality—half a dozen of those perhaps, of those alone, about the world; our friend was as sure of this, by the end of four minutes, as if he knew all about it.

After saying he would send him the book the young Lord indeed dropped that subject; he had asked where he might send it, and had had an "Oh, I shall remember!" on John's mention of an hotel; but he had made no further dash into literature, and it was ten to one that this would be the last the distinguished author might hear of the volume. Such again was a note of these high existences—that made one content to ask of them no whit of other consistency than that of carrying off the particular occasion, whatever it might be, in a dazzle of amiability and felicity and leaving *that* as a sufficient trace of their passage. Sought and achieved consistency was but an angular, a secondary motion; compared with the air of complete freedom it might have an effect of deformity. There was no placing this figure of radiant ease, for Berridge, in any relation that didn't appear not good enough—that is among the relations that hadn't been too good for Berridge himself. He was all right where he was; the great Gloriani somehow made that law; his house, with his supreme artistic position, was good enough for any one, and to-night in especial there were charming people, more charming than our friend could recall from any other scene, as the natural train or circle, as he might say, of such a presence. For an instant he thought he had got the face as a specimen of imperturbability watched, with wonder, across the hushed rattle of roulette at Monte-Carlo; but this quickly became as improbable as any question of a vulgar *table d'hote*, or a steam-boat deck, or a herd of fellow-pilgrims cicerone-led, or even an opera-box serving, during a performance, for frame of a type observed from the stalls. One placed young gods and goddesses only when one placed them on Olympus, and it met the case, always, that they were of Olympian race, and that they glimmered for one, at the best, through their silver cloud, like the visiting apparitions in an epic.

This was brief and beautiful indeed till something happened that gave it, for Berridge, on the spot, a prodigious extension—an extension really as prodigious, after a little, as if he had suddenly seen the silver clouds multiply and then the whole of Olympus presently open. Music, breaking upon the large air, enjoined immediate attention, and in a moment he was listening, with the rest of the company, to an eminent tenor, who stood by the piano; and was aware, with it, that his Englishman had turned away and that in the vast, rich, tapestried room where, in spite of figures and objects so numerous, clear spaces, wide vistas, and, as they might be called, becoming situations abounded, there had been from elsewhere, at the signal of unmistakable song, a rapid accession of guests. At first he but took this in, and the way that several young women, for whom seats had been found, looked charming in the rapt attitude; while even the men, mostly standing and grouped, "composed," in their stillness, scarce less impressively, under the sway of the divine voice. It ruled the scene, to the last intensity, and yet our young man's fine sense found still a resource in the range of the eyes, without sound or motion, while all the rest of consciousness was held down as by a hand mailed in silver. It was better, in this way, than the opera—John alertly thought of that: the composition sung might be Wagnerian, but no Tristram, no Iseult, no Parsifal and, no Kundry of them all could ever show, could ever "act" to the music, as our friend had thus the power of seeing his dear contemporaries of either sex (armoured *they* so otherwise than in cheap Teutonic tinsel!) just continuously and inscrutably sit to it.

It made, the whole thing together, an enchantment amid which he had in truth, at a given moment, ceased to distinguish parts—so that he was himself certainly at last soaring as high as the singer's voice and forgetting, in a lost gaze at the splendid ceiling, everything of the occasion but what his intelligence poured into it. This, as happened, was a flight so sublime that by the time he had dropped his eyes again a cluster of persons near the main door had just parted to give way to a belated lady who slipped in, through the gap made for her, and stood for some minutes full in his view. It was a proof of the perfect hush that no one stirred to offer her a seat, and her entrance, in her high grace, had yet been so noiseless that she could remain at once immensely exposed and completely unabashed. For Berridge, once more, if the scenic show before him so melted into the music, here precisely might have been the heroine herself advancing to the foot-lights at her cue. The interest deepened to a thrill, and everything, at the touch of his recognition of this personage, absolutely the most beautiful woman now present, fell exquisitely together and gave him what he had been wanting from the moment of his taking in his young Englishman.

It was there, the missing connection: her arrival had on the instant lighted it by a flash. Olympian herself, supremely, divinely Olympian, she had arrived, could *only* have arrived, for the one person present of really equal race, our young man's late converser, whose flattering demonstration might now stand for one of the odd extravagant forms taken by nervous impatience. This charming, this dazzling woman had been one member of the couple disturbed, to his intimate conviction, the autumn previous, on his being pushed by the officials, at the last moment, into a compartment of the train that was to take him from Cremona to Mantua—where, failing a stop, he had had to keep his place. The other member, by whose felt but unseized identity he had been haunted, was the unconsciously insolent form of guaranteed happiness he had just been engaged with. The sense of the admirable intimacy that, having taken its precautions, had not reckoned with his irruption—this image had remained with him; to say nothing of the interest of aspect of the associated figures, so stamped somehow with rarity, so beautifully distinct from the common occupants of padded corners, and yet on the subject of whom, for the romantic structure he was immediately to raise, he had not had a scrap of evidence.

If he had imputed to them conditions it was all his own doing: it came from his inveterate habit of abysmal imputation, the snatching of the ell wherever the inch peeped out, without which where would have been the tolerability of life? It didn't matter now what he had imputed—and he always held that his expenses of imputation were, at the worst, a compliment to those inspiring them. It only mattered that each of the pair had been then what he really saw each now—full, that is, of the pride of their youth and beauty and fortune and freedom, though at the same time particularly preoccupied: preoccupied, that is, with the affairs, and above all with the passions, of Olympus. Who had they been, and what? Whence had they come, whither were they bound, what tie united them, what adventure engaged, what felicity, tempered by what peril, magnificently, dramatically attended? These had been his questions, all so inevitable and so impertinent, at the time, and to the exclusion of any scruples over his not postulating an inane honeymoon, his not taking the "tie," as he should doubtless properly have done, for the mere blest matrimonial; and he now retracted not one of them, flushing as they did before him again with their old momentary life. To feel his two friends renewedly in presence—friends of the fleeting hour though they had but been, and with whom he had exchanged no sign save the vaguest of salutes on finally relieving them of his company—was only to be conscious that he hadn't, on the spot, done them, so to speak, half justice, and that, for his superior entertainment, there would be ever so much more of them to come.

II

It might already have been coming indeed, with an immense stride, when, scarce more than ten minutes later, he was aware that the distinguished stranger had brought the Princess straight across the room to speak to him. He had failed in the interval of any glimpse of their closer meeting; for the great tenor had sung another song and then stopped, immediately on which Madame Gloriani had made his pulse quicken to a different, if not to a finer, throb by hovering before him once more with the man in the world he most admired, as it were, looking at him over her shoulder. The man in the world he most admired, the greatest then of contemporary Dramatists— and bearing, independently, the name inscribed if not in deepest incision at least in thickest gilding on the rich recreative roll—this prodigious personage was actually to suffer "presentation" to him at the good lady's generous but ineffectual hands, and had in fact the next instant, left alone with him, bowed, in formal salutation, the massive, curly, witty head, so "romantic" yet so modern, so "artistic" and ironic yet somehow so civic, so Gallic yet somehow so cosmic, his personal vision of which had not hitherto transcended that of the possessor of a signed and framed photograph in a consecrated quarter of a writing-table.

It was positive, however, that poor John was afterward to remember of this conjunction nothing whatever but the fact of the great man's looking at him very hard, straight in the eyes, and of his not having himself scrupled to do as much, and with a confessed intensity of appetite. It was improbable, he was to recognise, that they had, for the few minutes, only stared and grimaced, like pitted boxers or wrestlers; but what had abode with him later on, none the less, was just the cherished memory of his not having so lost presence of mind as to fail of feeding on his impression. It was precious and precarious, that was perhaps all there would be of it; and his subsequent consciousness was quite to cherish this queer view of the silence, neither awkward nor empty nor harsh, but on the contrary quite charged and brimming, that represented for him his use, his unforgettable enjoyment in fact, of his opportunity. Had nothing passed in words? Well, no misery of murmured "homage," thank goodness; though something must have been said, certainly, to lead up, as they put it at the theatre, to John's having asked the head of the profession, before they separated, if he by chance knew who the so radiantly handsome young woman might be, the one who had so lately come in and who wore the pale yellow dress, of the strange tone, and the magnificent pearls. They must have separated soon, it was further to have been noted; since it was before the advance of the pair, their wonderful dazzling charge upon him, that he had distinctly seen the great man, at a distance again, block out from his sight the harmony of the faded gold and the pearls—to speak only of that—and plant himself there (the mere high Atlas-back of renown to Berridge now) as for communion with them. He had blocked everything out, to this tune, effectually; with nothing of the matter left for our friend meanwhile but that, as he had said, the beautiful lady was the Princess. What Princess, or the Princess of what?—our young man had afterward wondered; his companion's reply having lost itself in the prelude of an outburst by another vocalist who had approached the piano.

It was after these things that she so incredibly came to him, attended by her adorer—since he took it for absolute that the young Lord was her adorer, as who indeed mightn't be?—and scarce waiting, in her bright simplicity, for any form of introduction. It may thus be said in a word that this was the manner in which she made our hero's acquaintance, a satisfaction that she on the spot described to him as really wanting of late to her felicity. "I've read everything, you know, and 'The Heart of Gold' three times": she put it all immediately on that ground, while the young Lord now smiled, beside her, as if it were quite the sort of thing he had done too; and while, further, the author of the work yielded to the consciousness that whereas in general he had come at last scarce to be able to bear the iteration of those words, which affected him as a mere vain vocal convulsion, so not a breath of this association now attended them, so such a person as the Princess could make of them what she would.

Unless it was to be really what *he* would!—this occurred to him in the very thick of the prodigy, no single shade of possibility of which was less prodigious than any other. It was a declaration, simply, the admirable young woman was treating him to, a profession of "artistic sympathy"—for she was in a moment to use this very term that made for them a large, clear, common ether, an element all uplifted and rare, of which they could equally partake.

If she was Olympian—as in her rich and regular young beauty, that of some divine Greek mask over-painted say by Titian, she more and more appeared to him—this offered air was that of the gods themselves: she might have been, with her long rustle across the room, Artemis decorated, hung with pearls, for her worshippers, yet disconcerting them by having, under an impulse just faintly fierce, snatched the cup of gold from Hebe. It was to him, John Berridge, she thus publicly offered it; and it was his over-topping *confrere* of shortly before who was the worshipper most disconcerted. John had happened to catch, even at its distance, after these friends had joined him, the momentary deep, grave estimate, in the great Dramatist's salient watching eyes, of the Princess's so singular performance: the touch perhaps this, in the whole business, that made Berridge's sense of it most sharp. The sense of it as *prodigy* didn't in the least entail his feeling abject—any more, that is, than in the due dazzled degree; for surely there would have been supreme wonder in the eagerness of her exchange of mature glory for thin notoriety, hadn't it still exceeded everything that an Olympian of such race should have found herself bothered, as they said, to "read" at all—and most of all to read three times!

With the turn the matter took as an effect of this meeting, Berridge was more than once to find himself almost ashamed for her—since it seemed never to occur to her to be so for herself: he was jealous of the type where she might have been taken as insolently careless of it; his advantage (unless indeed it had been his ruin) being that he could inordinately reflect upon it, could wander off thereby into kinds of licence of which she was incapable. He hadn't, for himself, waited till now to be sure of what he would do were *he* an Olympian: he would leave his own stuff snugly unread, to begin with; that would be a beautiful start for an Olympian career. He should have been as unable to write those works in short as to make anything else of them; and he should have had no more arithmetic for computing fingers than any perfect-headed marble Apollo mutilated at the wrists. He should have consented to know but the grand personal adventure on the grand personal basis: nothing short of this, no poor cognisance of confusable, pettifogging things, the sphere of earth-grubbing questions and two-penny issues, would begin to be, on any side, Olympian enough.

Even the great Dramatist, with his tempered and tested steel and his immense "assured" position, even he was not Olympian: the look, full of the torment of earth, with which he had seen the Princess turn her back, and for such a purpose, on the prized privilege of his notice, testified sufficiently to that. Still, comparatively, it was to be said, the question of a personal relation with an authority so eminent on the subject of the passions—to say nothing of the rest of his charm—might have had for an ardent young woman (and the Princess was unmistakably ardent) the absolute attraction of romance: unless, again, prodigy of prodigies, she were looking for her romance very particularly elsewhere. Yet where could she have been looking for it, Berridge was to ask himself with private intensity, in a manner to leave her so at her ease for appearing to offer *him* everything?—so free to be quite divinely gentle with him, to hover there before him in all her mild, bright, smooth sublimity and to say: "I should be so very grateful if you'd come to see me."

There succeeded this a space of time of which he was afterward to lose all account, was never to recover the history; his only coherent view of it being that an interruption, some incident that kept them a while separate, had then taken place, yet that during their separation, of half an hour or whatever, they had still somehow not lost sight of each other, but had found their eyes meeting, in deep communion, all across the great peopled room; meeting and wanting to meet, wanting—it was the most extraordinary thing in the world for the suppression of stages, for confessed precipitate intensity—to use together every instant of the hour that might be left them. Yet to use it for what?—unless, like beautiful fabulous figures in some old-world legend, for the frankest and almost the crudest avowal of the impression they had made on each other. He couldn't have named, later on, any other person she had during this space been engaged with, any more than he was to remember in the least what he had himself ostensibly done, who had spoken to him, whom he had spoken to, or whether he hadn't just stood and publicly gaped or languished.

Ah, Olympians were unconventional indeed—that was a part of their high bravery and privilege; but what it also appeared to attest in this wondrous manner was that they could communicate to their chosen in three minutes, by the mere light of their eyes, the same shining cynicism. He was to wonder of course, tinglingly enough, whether he had really made an ass of himself, and there was this amount of evidence for it that there certainly *had* been a series of moments each one of which glowed with the lucid sense that, as she couldn't like him as much as *that* either for his acted clap-trap or for his printed verbiage, what it must come to was that she liked him, and to such a tune, just for himself and quite after no other fashion than that in which every goddess in the calendar had, when you came to look, sooner or later liked some prepossessing young shepherd. The question would thus have been, for him, with a still sharper eventual ache, of whether he positively *had*, as an effect of the miracle, been petrified, before fifty pair of eyes, to the posture of a prepossessing shepherd—and would perhaps have left him under the shadow of some such imputable fatuity if his consciousness hadn't, at a given moment, cleared up to still stranger things.

The agent of the change was, as quite congruously happened, none other than the shining youth whom he now seemed to himself to have been thinking of for ever so long, for a much longer time than he had ever in his life spent at an evening party, as the young Lord: which personage suddenly stood before him again, holding him up an odd object and smiling, as if in reference to it, with a gladness that at once struck our friend as almost too absurd for belief. The object was incongruous by reason of its being, to a second and less preoccupied glance, a book; and what had befallen Berridge within twenty minutes was that they—the Princess and he, that is—had got such millions of miles, or at least such thousands of years, away from *those* platitudes. The book, he found himself assuming, could only be *his* book (it seemed also to have a tawdry red cover); and there came to him memories, dreadfully false notes sounded so straight again by his new acquaintance, of certain altogether different persons who at certain altogether different parties had

Henry James

flourished volumes before him very much with that insinuating gesture, that arch expression, and that fell intention. The meaning of these things—of all possible breaks of the charm at such an hour!—was that he should "signature" the ugly thing, and with a characteristic quotation or sentiment: that was the way people simpered and squirmed, the way they mouthed and beckoned, when animated by such purposes; and it already, on the spot, almost broke his heart to see such a type as that of the young Lord brought, by the vulgarest of fashions, so low. This state of quick displeasure in Berridge, however, was founded on a deeper question—the question of how in the world he was to remain for himself a prepossessing shepherd if he should consent to come back to these base actualities. It was true that even while this wonderment held him, his aggressor's perfect good conscience had placed the matter in a slightly different light.

"By an extraordinary chance I've found a copy of my friend's novel on one of the tables here—I see by the inscription that she has presented it to Gloriani. So if you'd like to glance at it—!" And the young Lord, in the pride of his association with the eminent thing, held it out to Berridge as artlessly as if it had been a striking natural specimen of some sort, a rosy round apple grown in his own orchard, or an exceptional precious stone, to be admired for its weight and lustre. Berridge accepted the offer mechanically—relieved at the prompt fading of his worst fear, yet feeling in himself a telltale facial blankness for the still absolutely anomalous character of his friend's appeal. He was even tempted for a moment to lay the volume down without looking at it—only with some extemporised promise to borrow it of their host and take it home, to give himself to it at an easier moment. Then the very expression of his fellow-guests own countenance determined in him a different and a still more dreadful view; in fact an immediate collapse of the dream in which he had for the splendid previous space of time been living. The young Lord himself, in his radiant costly barbarism, figured far better than John Berridge could do the prepossessing shepherd, the beautiful mythological mortal "distinguished" by a goddess; for our hero now saw that his whole manner of dealing with his ridiculous tribute was marked exactly by the grand simplicity, the prehistoric good faith, as one might call it, of far-off romantic and "plastic" creatures, figures of exquisite Arcadian stamp, glorified rustics like those of the train of peasants in "A Winter's Tale," who thought nothing of such treasure-trove, on a Claude Lorrain sea-strand, as a royal infant wrapped in purple: something in that fabulous style of exhibition appearing exactly what his present demonstration might have been prompted by. "The Top of the Tree, by Amy Evans"— scarce credible words floating before Berridge after he had with an anguish of effort dropped his eyes on the importunate title-page—represented an object as alien to the careless grace of goddess-haunted Arcady as a washed-up "kodak" from a wrecked ship might have been to the appreciation of some islander of wholly unvisited seas. Nothing could have been more in the tone of an islander deplorably diverted from his native interests and dignities than the glibness with which John's own child of nature went on. "It's her pen-name, Amy Evans"—he couldn't have said it otherwise had he been a blue-chinned penny-a-liner; yet marking it with a disconnectedness of intelligence that kept up all the poetry of his own situation and only crashed into that of other persons. The reference put the author of "The Heart of Gold" quite into *his* place, but left the speaker absolutely free of Arcady. "Thanks awfully"—Berridge somehow clutched at that, to keep everything from swimming. "Yes, I should like to look at it," he managed, horribly grimacing now, he believed, to say; and there was in fact a strange short interlude after this in which he scarce knew what had become of any one or of anything; in which he only seemed to himself to stand alone in a desolate place where even its desolation didn't save him from having to stare at the greyest of printed pages. Nothing here helped anything else, since the stamped greyness didn't even in itself make it impossible his eyes should follow such sentences as: "The loveliness of the face, which was that of the glorious period in which Pheidias reigned supreme, and which owed its most exquisite note to that shell-like curl of the upper lip which always somehow recalls for us the smile with which windblown Astarte must have risen from the salt sea to which she owed her birth and her terrible moods; or it was too much for all the passionate woman in her, and she let herself go, over the flowering land that had been, but was no longer their love, with an effect of blighting desolation that might have proceeded from one of the more physical, though not more awful, convulsions of nature."

He seemed to know later on that other and much more natural things had occurred; as that, for instance, with now at last a definite intermission of the rare music that for a long time past, save at the briefest intervals, had kept all participants ostensibly attentive and motionless, and that in spite of its high quality and the supposed privilege of listening to it he had allowed himself not to catch a note of, there was a great rustling and shifting and vociferous drop to a lower plane, more marked still with the quick clearance of a way to supper and a lively dispersal of most of the guests. Hadn't he made out, through the queer glare of appearances, though they yet somehow all came to him as confused and unreal, that the Princess was no longer there, wasn't even only crowded out of his range by the immediate multiplication of her court, the obsequious court that the change of pitch had at once permitted to close round her; that Gloriani had offered her his arm, in a gallant official way, as to the greatest lady present, and that he was left with half a dozen persons more knowing than the others, who had promptly taken, singly or in couples, to a closer inspection of the fine small scattered treasures of the studio?

He himself stood there, rueful and stricken, nursing a silly red-bound book under his arm very much as if he might have been holding on tight to an upright stake, or to the nearest piece of furniture, during some impression of a sharp earthquake-shock or of an attack of dyspeptic dizziness; albeit indeed that he wasn't conscious of this absurd, this instinctive nervous clutch till the thing that was to be more wonderful than any yet suddenly flared up for him—the sight of the Princess again on the threshold of the room, poised there an instant, in her exquisite grace, for recovery of some one or of something, and then, at recognition of him, coming straight to him across the empty place as if he alone, and nobody and nothing else, were what she incredibly wanted. She was there, she was radiantly *at* him, as if she had known and loved him for ten years—ten years during which, however, she had never quite been able, in spite of undiscouraged attempts, to cure him, as goddesses *had* to cure shepherds, of his mere mortal shyness.

"Ah no, not *that* one!" she said at once, with her divine familiarity; for she had in the flash of an eye "spotted" the particular literary production he seemed so very fondly to have possessed himself of and against which all the Amy Evans in her, as she would doubtless have put it, clearly wished on the spot to discriminate. She pulled it away from him; he let it go; he scarce knew what was happening—only made out that she distinguished the right one, the one that should have been shown him, as blue or green or purple, and intimated that her other friend, her fellow-Olympian, as Berridge had thought of him from the first, really did too clumsily bungle matters, poor dear, with his officiousness over the red one! She went on really as if she had come for that, some such rectification, some such eagerness of reunion with dear Mr. Berridge, some talk, after all the tiresome music, of questions really urgent; while, thanks to the supreme strangeness of it, the high tide of golden fable floated him afresh, and her pretext and her plea, the queerness of her offered motive, melted away after the fashion of the enveloping clouds that do their office in epics and idylls. "You didn't perhaps know I'm Amy Evans," she smiled, "or even perhaps that I write in English—which I love, I assure you, as much as you can yourself do, and which gives one (doesn't it? for who should know if not you?) the biggest of publics. I 'just love'—don't they say?— your American millions; and all the more that they really *take* me for Amy Evans, as I've just wanted to be taken, to be loved too for myself, don't you know?—that they haven't seemed to try at all to 'go behind' (don't you say?) my poor dear little *nom de guerre*. But it's the new one, my last, 'The Velvet Glove,' that I should like you to judge me by—if such a *corvee* isn't too horrible for you to think of; though I admit it's a move straight in the romantic direction—since after all (for I might as well make a clean breast of it) it's dear old discredited romance that I'm most in sympathy with. I'll send you 'The Velvet Glove' to-morrow, if you *can* find half an hour for it; and then—and *then*—!" She paused as for the positive bright glory of her meaning.

It could only be so extraordinary, her meaning, whatever it was, that the need in him that would—whatever it was again!—meet it most absolutely formed the syllables on his lips as: "Will you be very, *very* kind to me?"

"Ah 'kind,' dear Mr. Berridge? 'Kind,'" she splendidly laughed, "is nothing to what—!" But she pulled herself up again an instant. "Well, to what I want to be! Just *see*," she said, "how I want to be!" It was exactly, he felt, what he couldn't *but* see—in spite of books and publics and pen-names, in spite of the really "decadent" perversity, recalling that of the most irresponsibly insolent of the old Romans and

Byzantines, that could lead a creature so formed for living and breathing her Romance, and so committed, up to the eyes, to the constant fact of her personal immersion in it and genius for it, the dreadful amateurish dance of ungrammatically scribbling it, with editions and advertisements and reviews and royalties and every other futile item: since what was more of the deep essence of throbbing intercourse itself than this very act of her having broken away from people, in the other room, to whom he was as nought, of her having, with her *cranerie* of audacity and indifference, just turned her back on them all as soon as she had begun to miss him? What was more of it than her having forbidden them, by a sufficient curt ring of her own supremely silver tone, to attempt to check or criticise her freedom, than her having looked him up, at his distance, under all the noses he had put out of joint, so as to let them think whatever they might—not of herself (much she troubled to care!) but of the new champion to be reckoned with, the invincible young lion of the day? What was more of it in short than her having perhaps even positively snubbed for him the great mystified Sculptor and the great bewildered Dramatist, treated to this queer experience for the first time of their lives?

It all came back again to the really great ease of really great ladies, and to the perfect facility of everything when once they were great enough. *That* might become the delicious thing to him, he more and more felt, as soon as it should be supremely attested; it was ground he had ventured on, scenically, representation-ally, in the artistic sphere, but without ever dreaming he should "realise" it thus in the social. Handsomely, gallantly just now, moreover, he didn't so much as let it occur to him that the social experience would perhaps on some future occasion richly profit further scenic efforts; he only lost himself in the consciousness of all she invited him to believe. It took licence, this consciousness, the next moment, for a tremendous further throb, from what she had gone on to say to him in so many words—though indeed the words were nothing and it was all a matter but of the implication that glimmered through them: "Do you *want* very much your supper here?" And then while he felt himself glare, for charmed response, almost to the point of his tears rising with it: "Because if you don't—!"

"Because if I don't—?" She had paused, not from the faintest shade of timidity, but clearly for the pleasure of making him press.

"Why shouldn't we go together, letting me drive you home?"

"You'll come home with me?" gasped John Berridge while the perspiration on his brow might have been the morning dew on a high lawn of Mount Ida.

"No—you had better come with *me*. That's what I mean; but I certainly will come to you with pleasure some time if you'll let me."

She made no more than that of the most fatuous of freedoms, as he felt directly he had spoken that it might have seemed to her; and before he had even time to welcome the relief of not having then himself, for beastly contrition, to make more of it, she had simply mentioned, with her affectionate ease, that she wanted to get away, that of the bores there she might easily, after a little, have too much, and that if he'd but say the word they'd nip straight out together by an independent door and be sure to find her motor in the court. What word he had found to say, he was afterward to reflect, must have little enough mattered; for he was to have kept, of what then occurred, but a single other impression, that of her great fragrant rustle beside him over the rest of the ample room and toward their nearest and friendliest resource, the door by which he had come in and which gave directly upon a staircase. This independent image was just that of the only other of his fellow-guests with whom he had been closely concerned; he had thought of him rather indeed, up to that moment, as the Princess's fellow-Olympian—but a new momentary vision of him seemed now to qualify it.

The young Lord had reappeared within a minute on the threshold, that of the passage from the supper-room, lately crossed by the Princess herself, and Berridge felt him there, saw him there, wondered about him there, all, for the first minute, without so much as a straight look at him. He would have come to learn the reason of his friend's extraordinary public demonstration—having more right to his curiosity, or his anxiety or whatever, than any one else; he would be taking in the remarkable appearances that thus completed it, and would perhaps be showing quite a different face for them, at the point they had reached, than any that would have hitherto consorted with the beautiful security of his own position. So much, on our own young man's part, for this first flush of a presumption that he might have stirred the germs of ire in a celestial breast; so much for the moment during which nothing would have induced him to betray, to a possibly rueful member of an old aristocracy, a vulgar elation or a tickled, unaccustomed glee. His inevitable second thought was, however, it has to be confessed, another matter, which took a different turn—for, frankly, all the conscious conqueror in him, as Amy Evans would again have said, couldn't forego a probably supreme consecration. He treated himself to no prolonged reach of vision, but there was something he nevertheless fully measured for five seconds—the sharp truth of the fact, namely, of how the interested observer in the doorway must really have felt about him. Rather disconcertingly, hereupon, the sharp truth proved to be that the most amused, quite the most encouraging and the least invidious of smiles graced the young Lord's handsome countenance—forming, in short, his final contribution to a display of high social candour unprecedented in our hero's experience. No, he wasn't jealous, didn't do John Berridge the honour to be, to the extent of the least glimmer of a spark of it, but was so happy to see his immortal mistress do what she liked that he could positively beam at the odd circumstance of her almost lavishing public caresses on a gentleman not, after all, of negligible importance.

Well, it was all confounding enough, but this indication in particular would have jostled our friend's grasp of the presented cup had he had, during the next ten minutes, more independence of thought. That, however, was out of the question when one positively felt, as with a pang somewhere deep within, or even with a smothered cry for alarm, one's whole sense of proportion shattered at a blow and ceasing to serve. "Not *straight*, and not too fast, shall we?" was the ineffable young woman's appeal to him, a few minutes later, beneath the wide glass porch-cover that sheltered their brief wait for their chariot of fire. It was there even as she spoke; the capped charioteer, with a great clean curve, drew up at the steps of the porch, and the Princess's footman, before rejoining him in front, held open the door of the car. She got in, and Berridge was the next instant beside her; he could only say: "As you like, Princess—where you will; certainly let us prolong it; let us prolong everything; don't let us have it over—strange and beautiful as it can only be!—a moment sooner than we must." So he spoke, in the security of their intimate English, while the perpendicular imperturbable *valet-de-pied*, white-faced in the electric light, closed them in and then took his place on the box where the rigid liveried backs of the two men, presented through the glass, were like a protecting wall; such a guarantee of privacy as might come—it occurred to Berridge's inexpugnable fancy—from a vision of tall guards erect round Eastern seraglios.

His companion had said something, by the time they started, about their taking a turn, their looking out for a few of the night-views of Paris that were so wonderful; and after that, in spite of his constantly prized sense of knowing his enchanted city and his way about, he ceased to follow or measure their course, content as he was with the particular exquisite assurance it gave him. *That* was knowing Paris, of a wondrous bland April night; that was hanging over it from vague consecrated lamp-studded heights and taking in, spread below and afar, the great scroll of all its irresistible story, pricked out, across river and bridge and radiant *place*, and along quays and boulevards and avenues, and around monumental circles and squares, in syllables of fire, and sketched and summarised, further and further, in the dim fire-dust of endless avenues; that was all of the essence of fond and thrilled and throbbing recognition, with a thousand things understood and a flood of response conveyed, a whole familiar possessive feeling appealed to and attested.

"From you, you know, it *would* be such a pleasure, and I think—in fact I'm sure—it would do so much for the thing in America." Had she gone on as they went, or had there been pauses of easy and of charmed and of natural silence, breaks and drops from talk, but only into greater confidence and sweetness?—such as her very gesture now seemed a part of; her laying her gloved hand, for emphasis, on the back of his own, which rested on his knee and which took in from the act he scarce knew what melting assurance. The emphasis, it was true—this came to him even while for a minute he held his breath—seemed rather that of Amy Evans; and if her talk, while they rolled, had been in the sense of these words (he had really but felt that they were shut intimately in together, all his consciousness, all his discrimination of meanings and indications being so deeply and so exquisitely merged in that) the case wasn't as surely and sublimely, as extravagantly, as fabulously romantic for him as his excited pulses had been seeming to certify. Her hand was there on his own, in precious living proof, and splendid Paris hung over them, as a consecrating canopy, her purple night embroidered with gold; yet he waited, something stranger still having glimmered for him, waited though she left her hand, which expressed emphasis and homage and tenderness, and anything else she liked indeed—since it was all then a matter of what he next heard and what he slowly grew cold as he took from her.

"You know they do it here so charmingly—it's a compliment a clever man is always so glad to pay a literary friend, and sometimes, in the case of a great name like yours, it renders such a service to a poor little book like mine!" She spoke ever so humbly and yet ever so gaily—and still more than before with this confidence of the sincere admirer and the comrade. That, yes, through his sudden sharpening chill, was what first became distinct for him; she was mentioning somehow her explanation and her conditions—her motive, in fine, disconcerting, deplorable, dreadful, in respect to the experience, otherwise so boundless, that he had taken her as having opened to him; and she was doing it, above all, with the clearest coolness of her general privilege. What in particular she was talking about he as yet, still holding his breath, wondered; it was something she wanted him to do for her—which was exactly what he had hoped, but something of what trivial and, heaven forgive them both, of what dismal order? Most of all, meanwhile, he felt the dire penetration of two or three of the words she had used; so that after a painful minute the quaver with which he repeated them resembled his-drawing, slowly, carefully, timidly, some barbed dart out of his flesh.

"A 'literary friend'?" he echoed as he turned his face more to her; so that, as they sat, the whites of her eyes, near to his own, gleamed in the dusk like some silver setting of deep sapphires.

It made her smile—which in their relation now was like the breaking of a cool air-wave over the conscious sore flush that maintained itself through his general chill. "Ah, of course you don't allow that I *am* literary—and of course if you're awfully cruel and critical and incorruptible you won't let it say for me what I so want it should!"

"Where are we, where, in the name of all that's damnably, of all that's grotesquely delusive, are we?" he said, without a sign, to himself; which was the form of his really being quite at sea as to what she was talking about. That uncertainty indeed he could but frankly betray by taking her up, as he cast about him, on the particular ambiguity that his voice perhaps already showed him to find most irritating. "Let it show? 'It,' dear Princess—?"

"Why, my dear man, let your Preface show, the lovely, friendly, irresistible log-rolling Preface that I've been asking you if you wouldn't be an angel and write for me."

He took it in with a deep long gulp—he had never, it seemed to him, had to swallow anything so bitter. "You've been asking me if I wouldn't write you a Preface?"

"To 'The Velvet Glove'—after I've sent it to you and you've judged if you really can. Of course I don't want you to perjure yourself; but"—and she fairly brushed him again, at their close quarters, with her fresh fragrant smile—"I do want you so to like me, and to say it all out beautifully and publicly." "You want me to like you, Princess?" "But, heaven help us, haven't you understood?" Nothing stranger could conceivably have been, it struck him—if he was right now—than this exquisite intimacy of her manner of setting him down on the other side of an abyss. It was as if she had lifted him first in her beautiful arms, had raised him up high, high, high, to do it, pressing him to her immortal young breast while he let himself go, and then, by some extraordinary effect of her native force and her alien quality, setting him down exactly where she wanted him to be— which was a thousand miles away from her. Once more, so preposterously face to face with her for these base issues, he took it all in; after which he felt his eyes close, for amazement, despair and shame, and his head, which he had some time before, baring his brow to the mild night, eased of its crush-hat, sink to confounded rest on the upholstered back of the seat. The act, the ceasing to see, and if possible to hear, was for the moment a retreat, an escape from a state that he felt himself fairly flatter by thinking of it as "awkward"; the state of really wishing that his humiliation might end, and of wondering in fact if the most decent course open to him mightn't be to ask her to stop the motor and let him down.

He spoke no word for a long minute, or for considerably more than that; during which time the motor went and went, now even somewhat faster, and he knew, through his closed eyes, that the outer lights had begun to multiply and that they were getting back somewhere into the spacious and decorative quarters. He knew this, and also that his retreat, for all his attitude as of accommodating thought, his air— *that* presently and quickly came to him—of having perhaps gathered himself in, for an instant, at her behest, to turn over, in his high ingenuity, some humbugging "rotten" phrase or formula that he might place at her service and make the note of such an effort; he became aware, I say, that his lapse was but a half-retreat, with her strenuous presence and her earnest pressure and the close cool respiration of her good faith absolutely timing the moments of his stillness and the progress of the car. Yes, it was wondrous well, he had all but made the biggest of all fools of himself, almost as big a one as *she* was still, to every appearance, in her perfect serenity, trying to make of him; and the one straight answer to it *would* be that he should reach forward and touch the footman's shoulder and demand that the vehicle itself should make an end.

That would be an answer, however, he continued intensely to see, only to inanely importunate, to utterly superfluous Amy Evans—not a bit to his at last exquisitely patient companion, who was clearly now quite taking it from him that what kept him in his attitude was the spring of the quick desire to oblige her, the charming loyal impulse to consider a little what he could do for her, say "handsomely yet conscientiously" (oh the loveliness!) before he should commit himself. She was enchanted—*that* seemed to breathe upon him; she waited, she hung there, she quite bent over him, as Diana over the sleeping Endymion, while all the conscientious man of letters in him, as she might so supremely have phrased it, struggled with the more peccable, the more muddled and "squared," though, for her own ideal, the so much more *banal* comrade. Yes, he could keep it up now—that is he could hold out for his real reply, could meet the rather marked tension of the rest of their passage as well as she; he should be able somehow or other to make his wordless detachment, the tribute of his ostensibly deep consideration of her request, a retreat in good order. She *was*, for herself, to the last point of her guileless fatuity, Amy Evans and an asker for "lifts," a conceiver of twaddle both in herself and in him; or at least, so far as she fell short of all this platitude, it was no fault of the really affecting folly of her attempt to become a mere magazine mortal after the only fashion she had made out, to the intensification of her self-complacency, that she might.

Nothing might thus have touched him more—if to be touched, beyond a certain point, hadn't been to be squared—than the way she failed to divine the bearing of his thoughts; so that she had probably at no one small crisis of her life felt so much a promise in the flutter of her own as on the occasion of the beautiful act she indulged in at the very moment, he was afterward to recognise, of their sweeping into her great smooth, empty, costly street—a desert, at that hour, of lavish lamplight and sculptured stone. She raised to her lips the hand she had never yet released and kept it there a moment pressed close against them; he himself closing his eyes to the deepest detachment he was capable of while he took in with a smothered sound of pain that this was the conferred bounty by which Amy Evans sought most expressively to encourage, to sustain and to reward. The motor had slackened and in a moment would stop; and meanwhile even after lowering his hand again she hadn't let it go. This enabled it, while he after a further moment roused himself to a more confessed consciousness, to form with his friend's a more active relation, to possess him of hers, in turn, and with an intention the straighter that her glove had by this time somehow come off. Bending over it without hinderance, he returned as firmly and fully as the application of all his recovered wholeness of feeling, under his moustache, might express, the consecration the bareness of his own knuckles had received; only after which it was that, still thus drawing out his grasp of her, and having let down their front glass by his free hand, he signified to the footman his view of their stopping short.

They had arrived; the high, closed *porte-cochere*, in its crested stretch of wall, awaited their approach; but his gesture took effect, the car pulled up at the edge of the pavement, the man, in an instant, was at the door and had opened it; quickly moving across the walk, the next moment, to press the bell at the gate. Berridge, as his hand now broke away, felt he had cut his cable; with which, after he had stepped out, he raised again the glass he had lowered and closed, its own being already down, the door that had released him. During these motions he had the sense of his companion, still radiant and splendid, but somehow momen-tarily suppressed, suspended, silvered over and celestially blurred, even as a summer moon by the loose veil of a cloud. So it was he saw her while he leaned for farewell on the open window-ledge; he took her in as her visible intensity of bright vagueness filled the circle that the interior of the car made for her. It was such a state as she would have been reduced to—he felt this, was certain of it—for the first time in her life; and it was he, poor John Berridge, after all, who would have created the condition.

"Good-night, Princess. I sha'n't see you again."

Vague was indeed no word for it—shine though she might, in her screened narrow niche, as with the liquefaction of her pearls, the glimmer of her tears, the freshness of her surprise. "You won't come in—when you've had no supper?"

He smiled at her with a purpose of kindness that could never in his life have been greater; and at first but smiled without a word. He presently shook his head, however—doubtless also with as great a sadness. "I seem to have supped to my fill, Princess. Thank you, I won't come in."

It drew from her, while she looked at him, a long low anxious wail. "And you won't do my Preface?"

"No, Princess, I won't do your Preface. Nothing would induce me to say a word in print about you. I'm in fact not sure I shall ever mention you in any manner at all as long as ever I live."

He had felt for an instant as if he were speaking to some miraculously humanised idol, all sacred, all jewelled, all votively hung about, but made mysterious, in the recess of its shrine, by the very thickness of the accumulated lustre. And "Then you don't like me—?" was the marvellous sound from the image.

"Princess," was in response the sound of the worshipper,

"Princess, I adore you. But I'm ashamed for you."

"Ashamed—?"

"You *are* Romance—as everything, and by what I make out every one, about you is; so what more do you want? Your Preface—the only one worth speaking of—was written long ages ago by the most beautiful imagination of man."

Humanised at least for these moments, she could understand enough to declare that she didn't. "I don't, I don't!"

"You don't need to understand. Don't attempt such base things. Leave those to us. Only live. Only be. *We'll* do the rest."

She moved over—she had come close to the window. "Ah, but Mr. Berridge—!"

He raised both hands; he shook them at her gently, in deep and soft deprecation. "Don't sound my dreadful name. Fortunately, however, you can't help yourself."

"Ah, *voyons!* I so want—!"

He repeated his gesture, and when he brought down his hands they closed together on both of hers, which now quite convulsively grasped the window-ledge. "Don't speak, because when you speak you really say things—!" "You are Romance," he pronounced afresh and with the last intensity of conviction and persuasion. "That's all you have to do with it," he continued while his hands, for emphasis, pressed hard on her own.

Their faces, in this way, were nearer together than ever, but with the effect of only adding to the vividness of that dire

Henry James

non-intelligence from which, all perversely and incalculably, her very beauty now appeared to gain relief. This made for him a pang and almost an anguish; the fear of her saying something yet again that would wretchedly prove how little he moved her perception. So his eyes, of remonstrant, of suppliant intention, met hers close, at the same time that these, so far from shrinking, but with their quite other swimming plea all bedimmed now, seemed almost to wash him with the tears of her failure. He soothed, he stroked, he reassured her hands, for tender conveyance of his meaning, quite as she had just before dealt with his own for brave demonstration of hers. It was during these instants as if the question had been which of them *could* most candidly and fraternally plead. Full but of that she kept it up. "Ah, if you'd only think, if you'd only try—!"

He couldn't stand it—she was capable of believing he had edged away, excusing himself and trumping up a factitious theory, because he hadn't the wit, hadn't the hand, to knock off the few pleasant pages she asked him for and that any proper Frenchman, master of the *metier*, would so easily and gallantly have promised. Should she so begin to commit herself he'd, by the immortal gods, anticipate it in the manner most admirably effective—in fact he'd even thus make her further derogation impossible. Their faces were so close that he could practise any rich freedom—even though for an instant, while the back of the chauffeur guarded them on that side and his own presented breadth, amplified by his loose mantle, filled the whole window-space, leaving him no observation from any quarter to heed, he uttered, in a deep-drawn final groan, an irrepressible echo of his pang for what might have been, the muffled cry of his insistence. "You *are* Romance!"—he drove it intimately, inordinately home, his lips, for a long moment, sealing it, with the fullest force of authority, on her own; after which, as he broke away and the car, starting again, turned powerfully across the pavement, he had no further sound from her than if, all divinely indulgent but all humanly defeated, she had given the question up, falling back to infinite wonder. He too fell back, but could still wave his hat for her as she passed to disappearance in the great floridly framed aperture whose wings at once came together behind her.

MORA MONTRAVERS

I

THEY were such extraordinary people to have been so odiously stricken that poor Traffle himself, always, at the best—though it was indeed just now at the worst—what his wife called horribly philosophic, fairly grimaced back, in private, at so flagrant a show of the famous, the provokedly vicious, "irony," the thing he had so often read about in clever stories, with which the usually candid countenance of their fate seemed to have begun of a sudden to bristle. Ah, that irony of fate often admired by him as a phrase and recognised as a truth—so that if he himself ever wrote a story it should certainly and most strikingly *be* about that— he fairly saw it leer at them now, could quite positively fancy it guilty of a low wink at them, in their trouble, out of that vast visage of the world that was made up for them of the separate stony stares or sympathising smirks presented by the circle of their friends. When he could get away from Jane he would pause in his worried walk—about the house or the garden, always, since he could now seldom leave her to brood alone for longer than that—and, while he shook his keys or his loose coin restlessly and helplessly in the pockets into which his hands had come to be inveterdeplorably, that any fledgling of their general nest (and Mora was but gone twenty-one and really clever with her brush) should *have* such a nature. It wasn't that, since her coming to them at fifteen, they had been ever, between themselves, at their ease about her—glossed over as everything had somehow come to be by the treacherous fact of her beauty. She had been such a credit to them that way that if it hadn't put them, as earnest observers, quite off their guard, the dazzle and charm of it appeared mostly to have misled their acquaintance. That was the worst cruelty for them, that with such a personal power to please she shouldn't, even on some light irregular line, have flown, as might have been conceived, higher. These things were dreadful, were even grotesque, to say; but what wasn't so now—after his difficult, his critical, his distinctly conclusive and, above all, as he secretly appraised it, his unexpectedly and absurdly interesting interview with Mr. Puddick? This passage, deplorably belated by Mora's own extraordinarily artful action, had but just taken place, and it had sent him back to Jane saddled with the queerest and most difficult errand of his life. He hadn't, however, on his return, at once sought her in the drawing-room—though her plan of campaign had been that they should fly their flag as high as ever, and, changing none of their refined habits, sit in that bow-windowed place of propriety, even as in a great glazed public cage, as much as ever—he had sneaked away again to tip-toe, with his pensive private humour, over the whole field; observing in her society, for the most part, the forms of black despair and grim participation, if even at the same time avoiding inconsiderate grossness; but at bottom, since his moments with Puddick, almost ready to take, as a man of the world, the impartial, the detached, in fact—hang it!—even the amused view. It hadn't as yet made a shade of difference in his tone that Mora was Jane's niece, and not even her very own, but only the child of her half-sister, whose original union with Malcolm Mon-travers had moreover made a break between them that had waited for healing till after the ill-starred husband's death and the eve of that of the perfectly disillusioned wife; but in these slightly rueful, though singularly remedial, dips into thoughtful solitude he had begun at last to treat himself to luxuries that he could feel he was paying for. Mora was, accurately speaking, no sharer of his blood, and he absolutely denied her the right not alone socially to dishonour, but, beyond a mere ruffle of the surface, morally to discompose him; mixed with which rather awkwardly, not to say perhaps a bit perversely, was the sense that as the girl was showing up, unmistakably, for one of the most curious of "cases"—the term Puddick himself had used about her—she wouldn't be unlikely to reward some independent, some intelligent notice.

He had never from the first, to do himself—or to do *her*—justice, felt he had really known her, small, cool, supposedly childish, yet not a bit confiding, verily not a bit appealing, presence as she was; but clearly he should know her now, and to do so might prove indeed a job. Not that he wanted to be *too* cold-blooded about her—that is in the way of enlightened appreciation, the detachment of the simply scandalised state being another matter; for this was somehow to leave poor Jane, and poor Jane's gloom of misery, in the lurch. But once safely back from the studio, Puddick's own—where he hadn't been sure, upon his honour, that some coarse danger mightn't crop up—he indulged in a surreptitious vow that if any "fun," whether just freely or else more or less acutely speaking, was to come of the matter, he'd be blamed if he'd be wholly deprived of it. The possibility of an incalculable sort of interest—in fact, quite a refined sort, could there be refinement in such doings—had somehow come out with Puddick's at once saying: "Certainly sir, I'll marry her if you and Mrs. Truffle absolutely insist—and if Mora herself (the great point!) can be brought round to look at it in that way. But I warn you that if I do, and that if she makes that concession, I shall probably lose my hold of her—which won't be best, you know, for any one concerned.

You don't suppose I don't *want* to make it all right, do you?" the surprising young man had gone on. "The question's only of what *is* right—or what will be if we keep our heads and take time—with such an extraordinary person as Mora, don't you see? to deal with. You must grant me," Mr. Puddick had wound up, "that she's a rum case."

II

What he had first felt, of course, was the rare coolness of it,
the almost impudent absence of any tone of responsibility;
which had begun by seeming to make the little painter-man's
own case as "rum," surely, as one could imagine it. He had
gone, poor troubled Traffle, after the talk, straight to his own
studio, or to the rather chill and vague, if scrupulously neat,
pavilion at the garden-end, which he had put up eight years
ago in the modest hope that it would increasingly inspire
him; since it wasn't making preparations and invoking
facilities that constituted swagger, but, much rather,
behaving as if one's powers could boldly dispense with them.
He was certain Jane would come to him there on hearing of
him from the parlour-maid, to whom he had said a word in
the hall. He wasn't afraid—no—of having to speak a little as
he felt; but, though well aware of his wife's impatience, he
wasn't keen, either, for any added intensity of effort to
abound only in Mrs. Traffle's sense. He required space and
margin, he required a few minutes' time, to say to himself
frankly that this dear dismal lady *had* no sense—none at
least of their present wretched question—that was at all
worth developing: since he of course couldn't possibly
remark it to poor Jane. He had perhaps never remarked for
his own private benefit so many strange things as between
the moment of his letting himself again into the perpetually
swept and garnished temple of his own perfunctory aesthetic
rites, where everything was ready to his hand and only that
weak tool hung up, and his glimpse of Jane, from the smaller
window, as she came down the garden walk. Pud-dick's
studio had been distinctly dirty, and Puddick himself, from
head to foot, despite his fine pale little face and bright,
direct, much more searching than shifting eyes, almost as
spotty as the large morsel of rag with which he had so oddly
begun to rub his fingers while standing there to receive

Mora's nearest male relative; but the canvas on his easel, the thing that even in the thick of his other adventure was making so straight a push for the Academy, almost embarrassed that relative's eyes, not to say that relative's conscience, by the cleanness of its appeal. Traffle hadn't come to admire his picture or to mark how he didn't muddle where not muddling was vital; he had come to denounce his conduct, and yet now, perhaps most of all, felt the strain of having pretended so to ignore what would intensely have interested him. Thanks to this barren artifice, to the after-effect of it on his nerves, his own preposterous place, all polish and poverty, pointed such a moral as he had never before dreamed of. Spotless it might be, unlike any surface or aspect presented under the high hard Puddick north-light, since it showed no recording trace, no homely smear—since it had had no hour of history. That was the way truth showed and history came out—in spots: by them, and by nothing else, you knew the real, as you knew the leopard, so that the living creature and the living life equally had to have them. Stuffed animals and weeping women were—well, another question. He had gathered, on the scene of his late effort, that Mora didn't weep, that she was still perfectly pleased with her shocking course; her complacency indeed remained at such a pitch as to make any question of her actual approach, on whatever basis, or any rash direct challenge of her, as yet unadvisable. He was at all events, after another moment, in presence of Jane's damp severity; *she* never ceased crying, but her tears froze as they fell—though not, unfortunately, to firm ice, any surface that would bear the weight of large argument. The only thing for him, none the less, was to carry the position with a rush, and he came at once to the worst.

"He'll do it—he's willing; but he makes a most striking point—I mean given the girl as we know her and as he of course by this time must. He keeps his advantage, he thinks, by not forcing the note—don't you see?" Traffle himself—

under the quick glow of his rush—actually saw more and more. "He's feeling his way—he used that expression to me; and again I haven't to tell you, any more than he really had to tell me, that with Mora one has to sit tight. He puts on us, in short, the responsibility."

He had felt how more than ever her "done" yellow hair—done only in the sense of an elaborately unbecoming conformity to the spasmodic prescriptions, undulations and inflations of the day, not in that of any departure from its pale straw-coloured truth—was helped by her white invalidical shawl to intensify those reminders of their thin ideals, their bloodless immunity, their generally compromised and missed and forfeited frankness, that every other feature of their domestic scene had just been projecting for him. "Responsibility—we responsible?" She gaped with the wonder of it.

"I mean that we should be if anything were to happen by our trying to impose on her *our* view of her one redemption. I give it you for his own suggestion—and thereby worth thinking of."

But Jane could take nothing in. "He suggests that he needn't marry her, and you agree with him? Pray what is there left to 'happen,'" she went on before he could answer, "after her having happened so completely to disgrace herself?"

He turned his back a moment—he had shortly before noticed a framed decoration, a "refined" Japanese thing that gave accent, as he would have said, to the neatness of his mouse-grey wall, and that needed straightening. Those spare apprehensions had somehow, it was true, suddenly been elbowed out of his path by richer ones; but he obeyed his old habit. "She can leave him, my dear; that's what she can do—and not, you may well believe, to come back to us."

"If she *will* come I'll take her—even now," said Jane Traffle; "and who can ask of me more than that?"

He slid about a little, sportively, on his polished floor, as if he would have liked to skate, while he vaguely, inaudibly hummed. "Our difficulty is that she doesn't ask the first blessed thing of us. We've been, you see, too stupid about her. Puddick doesn't say it, but he knows it—that I felt She feels what she is—and so does he."

"What she is? She's an awful little person"—and Mrs. Traffle stated it with a cold finality she had never yet used.

"Well then, that's what she feels!—even though it's probably not the name she employs in connection with it. She has tremendously the sense of life."

"That's bad," cried Jane, "when you haven't—not even feebly!—the sense of decency."

"How do you know, my dear," he returned, "when you've never had it?" And then as she but stared, since he couldn't mean she hadn't the sense of decency, he went on, really quite amazed at himself: "People must have both if possible, but if they can only have one I'm not sure that that one, as we've had it—not at all 'feebly,' as you say!—is the better of the two. What do we know about the sense of life—when it breaks out with real freedom? It has never broken out here, my dear, for long enough to leave its breath on the window-pane. But they've got it strong down there in Puddick's studio."

She looked at him as if she didn't even understand his language, and she flopped thereby into the trap set for her by a single word. "Is she living *in* the studio?"

He didn't avoid her eyes. "I don't know where she's living."

"And do I understand that you didn't ask him?"

"It was none of my business—I felt that there in an unexpected way; I couldn't somehow *not* feel it—and I suggest, my dear, accordingly, that it's also none of yours. I wouldn't answer, if you really want to know," he wound up, hanging fire an instant, but candidly bringing it out—"I wouldn't answer, if you really want to know, for their relations."

Jane's eyebrows mounted and mounted. "Whoever in the world would?"

He waited a minute, looking off at his balanced picture—though not as if now really seeing it. "I'm not talking of what the vulgar would say—or *are* saying, of course, to their fill. I'm not talking of what those relations may be. I'm talking—well," he said, "of what they mayn't."

"You mean they may be innocent?"

"I think it possible. They're, as he calls it, a 'rum' pair. They're not like us."

"If we're not like them," she broke in, "I grant you I hope not"

"We've no imagination, you see," he quietly explained—"whereas they have it on tap, for the sort of life they lead down there, all the while." He seemed wistfully to figure it out. "For us only one kind of irregularity is possible—for them, no doubt, twenty kinds."

Poor Jane listened this time—and so intently that after he

had spoken she still rendered his obscure sense the tribute of a wait. "You think it's possible she's not living with him?"

"I think anything possible."

"Then what in the world did she want?"

"She wanted in the first place to get away from us. We didn't like her—"

"Ah, we never let her see it!"—Jane could triumphantly make *that* point.

It but had for him, however, an effect of unconscious comedy. "No, that was it—and she wanted to get away from everything we did to prevent her; from our solemn precautions *against* her seeing it We didn't understand her, or we should have understood how much she must have wanted to. We were afraid of her in short, and she wanted not to see our contortions over it. Puddick isn't beautiful—though he has a fine little head and a face with some awfully good marks; but he's a Greek god, for statuesque calm, compared with us. He isn't afraid of her."

Jane drew herself elegantly up. "I understood you just now that it's exactly what he *is*!"

Traffie reflected. "That's only for his having to deal with her in our way. Not if he handles her in his own."

"And what, pray, is his own?"

Traffle, his hands in his pockets, resumed his walk, touching with the points of his shoes certain separations between the highly-polished planks of his floor. "Well, why should we have to know?"

Henry James

"Do you mean we're to wash our hands of her?"

He only circulated at first—but quite sounding a low whistle of exhilaration. He felt happier than for a long time; broken as at a blow was the formation of ice that had somehow covered, all his days, the whole ground of life, what he would have called the things under. There they were, the things under. He could see them now; which was practically what he after a little replied. "It will be so interesting." He pulled up, none the less, as he turned, before her poor scared and mottled face, her still suffused eyes, her "dressed" head parading above these miseries.

She vaguely panted, as from a dance through bush and briar. "But *what*, Sidney, will be?"

"To see what becomes of her. Without our muddling." Which was a term, however, that she so protested against his use of that he had on the spot, with more kindness than logic, to attenuate, admitting her right to ask him who could do less—less than take the stand she proposed; though indeed coming back to the matter that evening after dinner (they never really got away from it; but they had the consciousness now of false starts in other directions, followed by the captive returns that were almost as ominous of what might still be before them as the famous tragic *rentree* of Louis XVI and Marie Antoinette from Varennes); when he brought up, for their common relief, the essential fact of the young woman's history as they had suffered it to shape itself: her coming to them bereft and homeless, addressed, packed and registered after the fashion of a postal packet; their natural flutter of dismay and apprehension, but their patient acceptance of the charge; the five flurried governesses she had had in three years, who had so bored her and whom she had so deeply disconcerted; the remarkable disposition for drawing and daubing that she had shown from the first and that had led them to consent to her haunting of a class in town, that had made her acquainted with the as yet wholly undistinguished young artist, Walter Puddick, who, with a couple of other keen and juvenile adventurers of the brush, "criticised," all at their ease, according to the queer new licence of the day, and with nobody to criticise *them*, eighty supposed daughters of gentlemen; the uncontrolled spread of her social connection in London, on the oddest lines, as a proof of this prosecution of her studies; her consequent prolonged absences, her strange explanations and deeper duplicities, and presently her bolder defiances; with her staying altogether, at last, one fine day, under pretext of a visit at Highgate, and writing them at the end of a week, during which they had been without news of her, that her visit was to Mr. Puddick and his "set," and was likely to be of long duration, as he was "looking after her," and there were plenty of people in the set to help, and as she, above all, wanted nothing more: nothing more, of course, than her two hundred and seventy a year, the scant remainder of her mother's fortune that she had come into the use of, under that battered lady's will, on her eighteenth birthday, and through which her admirers, every member of the set, no doubt, wouldn't have found her least admirable. Puddick wouldn't be paying for her, by the blessing of heaven—*that*, Traffle recognised, would have been ground for anything; the case rather must be the other way round. She was "treating" the set, probably, root and branch—magnificently; so no wonder she was having success and liking it. Didn't Jane recognise, therefore, how in the light of this fact almost any droll *different* situation—different from the common and less edifying turn of such affairs—might here prevail? He could imagine even a fantastic delicacy; not on the part of the set at large perhaps, but on that of a member or two.

What Jane most promptly recognised, she showed him in answer to this, was that, with the tone he had so extraordinarily begun to take on the subject, his choice of terms left her staring. Their ordeal would have to be different indeed from anything she had yet felt it for it to affect her as droll, and Mora's behaviour to repudiate at every point and in some scarce conceivable way its present appearance for it to strike her either as delicate or as a possible cause of delicacy. In fact she could have but her own way—Mora was a monster.

"Well," he laughed—quite brazen about it now—"if she is it's because she has paid for it! Why the deuce did her stars, unless to make her worship gods entirely other than Jane Traffle's, rig her out with a name that puts such a premium on adventures? 'Mora Montravers'—it paints the whole career for you. She *is*, one does feel, her name; but how couldn't she be? She'd dishonour it and its grand air if she weren't."

"Then by that reasoning you admit," Mrs. Traffle returned with more of an argumentative pounce than she had perhaps ever achieved in her life, "that she is misconducting herself."

It pulled him up but ten seconds. "It isn't, love, that she's misconducting herself—it's that she's conducting, positively, and by her own lights doubtless quite responsibly, Miss Montravers through the preappointed circle of that young lady's experience." Jane turned on this a desolate back; but he only went on. "It would have been better for us perhaps if she could have been a Traffle—but, failing that, I think I should, on the ground that sinning at all one should sin boldly, have elected for Montravers outright. That *does* the thing—it gives the unmistakable note. And if 'Montravers' made it probable 'Mora'—don't you see, dearest?—made it sure. Would you *wish* her to change to Puddick?" This brought her round again, but as the affirmative hadn't quite leaped to her lips he found time to continue. "Unless indeed they can make some arrangement by which he takes *her* name. Perhaps we can work it that way!"

His suggestion was thrown out as for its positive charm; but Jane stood now, to do her justice, as a rock. "She's doing something that, surely, no girl in the world ever did before— in preferring, as I so strangely understand you, that her lover *shouldn't* make her the obvious reparation. But is her reason her dislike of his vulgar name?"

"That has no weight for *you*, Jane?" Traffle asked in reply.

Jane dismally shook her head. "Who, indeed, as you say, are we? Her reason—if it is her reason—is vulgarer still."

He didn't believe it could be Mora's reason, and though he had made, under the impression of the morning, a brave fight, he had after reflection to allow still for much obscurity in their question. But he had none the less retained his belief in the visibly uncommon young man, and took occasion to make of his wife an inquiry that hadn't hitherto come up in so straight a form and that sounded of a sudden rather odd. "Are you at all *attached* to her? Can you give me your word for *that?*"

She faced him again like a waning wintry moon. "Attached to Mora? Why she's my sister's child."

"Ah that, my dear, is no answer! Can you assure me on your honour that you're conscious of anything you can call real affection for her?"

Jane blankly brooded. "What has that to do with it?"

"I think it has everything. If we don't feel a tenderness."

"*You* certainly strike me as feeling one!" Mrs. Traffic sarcastically cried.

He weighed it, but to the effect of his protesting. "No, not enough for me to demand of her to marry to spare my sensibility."

His wife continued to gloom. "What is there in what she has done to *make* us tender?"

"Let us admit then, if there's nothing, that it has made us tough! Only then we must be tough. If we're having the strain and the pain of it let us also have the relief and the fun."

"Oh the 'fun'!" Jane wailed; but adding soon after: "If she'll marry him I'll forgive her."

"Ah, that's not enough!" he pronounced as they went to bed.

III

Yet he was to feel too the length that even forgiving her would have to go—for Jane at least—when, a couple of days later, they both, from the drawing-room window, saw, to their liveliest astonishment, the girl alight at the gate. She had taken a fly from the station, and their attention caught her as she paused apparently to treat with the cabman of the question of his waiting for her or coming back. It seemed settled in a moment that he should wait; he didn't remount his box, and she came in and up the garden-path. Jane had already flushed, and with violence, at the apparition, and in reply to her companion's instant question had said: "Yes, I'll see her if she has come back."

"Well, she *has* come back."

"She's keeping her cab—she hasn't come to stay." Mrs. Traffle had gained a far door of retreat.

"You won't speak to her?"

"Only if she has come to stay. *Then*—volumes!"

He had remained near the window, held fast there by the weight of indefinite obligation that his wife's flight from the field shifted to his shoulders. "But if she comes back to stay what can Puddick do?"

This kept her an instant. "To stay till he marries her is what I mean."

"Then if she asks for you—as she only must—am I to tell her that?"

Flushed and exalted, her hand on the door, Jane had for this question a really grand moment. "Tell her that if he will she shall come in—with your assent—for my four hundred."

"Oh, oh!" he ambiguously sounded while she whisked away and the door from the hall was at the same time thrown open by the parlour-maid. "Miss Montravers!" announced, with a shake of anguish, that domestic, whose heightened colour and scared eyes conformed to her mistress's example. Traffle felt his own cheek, for that matter, unnaturally glow, and the very first of his observations as Mora was restored to his sight might have been that she alone of them all wore her complexion with no difference. There was little doubt moreover that this charming balance of white and pink couldn't have altered but to its loss; and indeed when they were left alone the whole immediate effect for him of the girl's standing there in immediate bright silence was that of her having come simply to reaffirm her extraordinary prettiness. It might have been just to say: "You've thought, and you think, all sorts of horrible things about me, but observe how little my appearance matches them, and in fact keep up coarse views if you can in the light of my loveliness." Yet it wasn't as if she had changed, either, even to the extent of that sharper emphasis: he afterward reflected, as he lived over this passage, that he must have taken for granted in her, with the life she was leading, so to call it, some visibility of boldness, some significant surface—of which absurd supposition her presence, at the end of three minutes, had disabused him to the point of making all the awkwardness his and leaving none at all for her. That was a side of things, the awkward, that she clearly meant never again to recognise in conversation—though certainly from the first, ever, she had brushed it by lightly enough. She was in truth exactly the same—except for her hint that they might have forgotten how pretty she *could* be; and he further made sure she would incur neither pains nor costs for any new attempt on them. The Mora they had always taken her for would serve her perfectly still; that young woman was bad enough, in all conscience, to hang together through anything that might yet happen.

So much he was to feel she had conveyed, and that it was the little person presenting herself, at her convenience, on these terms who had been all the while, in their past, their portentous inmate—since what had the portent been, by the same token, but exactly of this? By the end of three minutes more our friend's sole thought was to conceal from her that he had looked for some vulgar sign—such as, reported to Wimbledon tea-tables, could be confidentially mumbled about: he was almost as ashamed of that elderly innocence as if she had caught him in the fact of disappointment at it. Meanwhile she had expressed her errand very simply and serenely. "I've come to see you because I don't want to lose sight of you—my being no longer with you is no reason for that." She was going to ignore, he saw—and she would put it through: she was going to ignore everything that suited her, and the quantity might become prodigious. Thus it would rest upon *them*, poor things, to disallow, if they must, the grace of these negatives—in which process she would watch them flounder without help. It opened out before him—a vertiginous view of a gulf; the abyss of what the ignoring would include for the convenient general commerce; of what might lie behind, in fine, should the policy foreshadow the lurking quantity.

He knew the vague void for one he should never bridge, and that to put on emphasis where Mora chose to neglect it would be work only for those who "gathered samphire" like the unfortunates in "King Lear," or those who, by profession, planted lightning-rods at the tips of tremendous towers. He was committed to pusillanimity, which would yet have to figure for him, before he had done with it, he knew, as a gallant independence, by letting ten minutes go without mention of Jane. Mora had put him somehow into the position of having to explain that her aunt wouldn't see her—precisely that was the mark of the girl's attitude. But he'd be hanged if he'd do anything of the sort.

It was therefore like giving poor Jane basely away, his not, to any tune, speaking for her—and all the more that their visitor sat just long enough to let his helplessness grow and reach perfection. By this facility it was he who showed—and for her amusement and profit—all the change she kept him from imputing to herself. He presented her—she held him up to himself as presenting her—with a new uncle, made over, to some loss of dignity, on purpose for her; and nothing could less have suited their theory of his right relation than to have a private understanding with her at his wife's expense. However, gracefully grave and imperturbable, inimitably armed by her charming correctness, as she sat there, it would be her line in life, he was certain, to reduce many theories, solemn Wimbledon theories about the scandalous person, to the futility of so much broken looking-glass. Not naming her aunt—since *he* didn't—she had of course to start, for the air of a morning call, some other day or two; she asked for news of their few local friends quite as if these good people mightn't ruefully have "cut" her, by what they had heard, should they have met her out on the road. She spoke of Mr. Puddick with perfect complacency, and in particular held poor Traffle very much as some master's fiddle-bow might have made him hang on the semi-tone of a silver string when she referred to the visit he had paid the artist and to the latter's having wondered whether he liked what he saw. She liked, more and more, Mora intimated, what was offered to her own view; Puddick was going to do, she was sure, such brilliant work—so that she hoped immensely he would come again. Traffle found himself, yes—it was positive—staying his breath for this; there was in fact a moment, that of her first throwing off her free "Puddick," when it wouldn't have taken much more to make him almost wish that, for rounded perfection, she'd say "Walter" at once. He would scarce have guaranteed even that there hadn't been just then some seconds of his betraying that imagination in the demoralised eyes that her straight, clear, quiet beams sounded and sounded, against every presumption of what might have been. What essentially happened, at any rate, was that by the time she went she had not only settled him in the sinister attitude of having lost all interest in her aunt, but had made him give her for the profane reason of it that he was gaining so much in herself.

He rushed in again, for that matter, to a frank clearance the moment he had seen the girl off the premises, attended her, that is, back to her fly. He hadn't at this climax remarked to her that she must come again—which might have meant either of two or three incoherencies and have signified thereby comparatively little; he had only fixed on her a rolling eye—for it rolled, he strangely felt, without leaving her; which had the air of signifying heaven knew what. She took it, clearly, during the moment she sat there before her start, for the most rather than for the least it might mean; which again made him gape with the certitude that ever thereafter she would make him seem to have meant what she liked. She had arrived in a few minutes at as wondrous a recipe or as quick an inspiration for this as if she had been a confectioner using some unprecedented turn of the ladle for some supersubtle cream. He was a proved conspirator from that instant on, which was practically what he had qualified Jane, within ten minutes—if Jane had only been refreshingly sharper—to pronounce him. For what else in the world did it come to, his failure of ability to attribute any other fine sense to Mora's odd "step" than the weird design of just giving them a lead? They were to leave her alone, by her sharp prescription, and she would show them once for all how to do it. Cutting her dead wasn't leaving her alone, any idiot could do that; conversing with her affably was the privilege she offered, and the one he had so effectually embraced—he made a clean breast of this—that he had breathed to her no syllable of the message left with him by her aunt.

"Then you mean," this lady now inquired, "that I'm to go and call upon her, at that impossible place, just as if she were the pink of propriety and we had no exception whatever to take to her conduct? Then you mean," Mrs. Traffle had pursued with a gleam in her eye of more dangerous portent than any he had ever known himself to kindle there—"then you mean that I'm to grovel before a chit of a creature on whom I've lavished every benefit, and to whom I've actually offered every indulgence, and who shows herself, in return for it all, by what I make out from your rigmarole, a fiend of insolence as well as of vice?"

The danger described by Sidney Traffle was not that of any further act of violence from Jane than this freedom of address to him, unprecedented in their long intercourse—this sustained and, as he had in a degree to allow, not unfounded note of sarcasm; such a resort to which, on his wife's part, would, at the best, mark the prospect for him, in a form flushed with novelty, of much conscious self-discipline. What looked out of her dear foolish face, very much with the effect of a new and strange head boldly shown at an old and familiar pacific window, was just the assurance that he might hope for no abashed sense in her of differing from him on all this ground as she had never differed on any. It was as if now, unmistakably, she *liked* to differ, the ground being her own and he scarce more than an unwarranted poacher there. Of course it *was* her own, by the fact, first, of Mora's being her, not his, sister's child; and, second, by all the force with which her announced munificence made it so. He took a moment to think how he could best meet her challenge, and then reflected that there was, happily, nothing like the truth—*his* truth, of which it was the insidious nature to prevail. "What she wanted, I make out, was but to give us the best pleasure she could think of. The pleasure, I mean, of our not only recognising how little we need worry about her, but of our seeing as well how pleasant it may become for us to keep in touch with her."

These words, he was well aware, left his wife—given her painful narrowness—a bristling quiver of retorts to draw from; yet it was not without a silent surprise that he saw her, with her irritated eyes on him, extract the bolt of finest point. He had rarely known her to achieve that discrimination before. "The pleasure then, in her view, you 'make out'—since you make out such wonders!—is to be all for us only?"

He found it fortunately given him still to smile. "That will depend, dear, on our appreciating it enough to make things agreeable to *her* in order to get it. But as she didn't inquire for you," he hastened to add, "I don't—no I don't—advise your going to see her *even* for the interest I speak of!" He bethought himself. "We must wait a while."

"Wait till she gets worse?"

He felt after a little that he should be able now always to command a kindly indulgent tone. "I'll go and see her if you like."

"Why in the world should I like it? Is it your idea—for the pleasure you so highly appreciate, and heaven knows what you mean by it!—to cultivate with her a free relation of your own?"

"No"—he promptly returned—"I suggest it only as acting *for* you. Unless," he went on, "you decidedly wish to act altogether for yourself."

For some moments she made no answer; though when she at last spoke it was as if it *were* an answer. "I shall send for Mr. Puddick."

"And whom will you send?"

"I suppose I'm capable of a note," Jane replied.

"Yes, or you might even telegraph. But are you sure he'll come?"

"Am I sure, you mean," she asked, "that his companion will let him? I can but try, at all events, and shall at any rate have done what I can."

"I think he's afraid of her—"

Traffle had so begun, but she had already taken him up. "And you're not, you mean—and that's why you're so eager?"

"Ah, my dear, my dear?" He met it with his strained grimace. "Let us by all means," he also, however, said, "have him if we can."

On which it was, for a little, that they strangely faced each other. She let his accommodation lie while she kept her eyes on him, and in a moment she had come up, as it were, elsewhere. "If I thought you'd see her—!"

"That I'd see her?"—for she had paused again.

"See her and go on with her—well, without my knowledge," quavered poor Jane, "I assure you you'd seem to me even worse than her. So will you promise me?" she ardently added.

"Promise you what, dear?" He spoke quite mildly.

"Not to see her in secret—which I believe would kill me."

"Oh, oh, oh, love!" Traffle smiled while she positively glared.

IV

Three days having elapsed, however, he had to feel that things had considerably moved on his being privileged to hear his wife, in the drawing-room, where they entertained Mr. Puddick at tea, put the great question straighter to that visitor than he himself, Sidney Traffle, could either have planned or presumed to do. Flushed to a fever after they had beat about the bush a little, Jane didn't flinch from her duty. "What I want to know in plain terms, if you please, is whether or no you're Mora's lover?" "Plain terms"—she did have inspirations! so that under the shock he turned away, humming, as ever, in his impatience, and, the others being seated over the vain pretence of the afternoon repast, left the young man to say what he might. It was a fool's question, and there was always a gape for the wisest (the greater the wisdom and the greater the folly) in any apprehension of such. As if he were going to say, remarkable Puddick, not less remarkable in his way than Mora—to say, that is, anything that would suit Jane; and as if it didn't give her away for a goose that she should assume he was! Traffle had never more tiptoed off to the far end of the room, whether for pretence of a sudden interest in his precious little old Copley Fielding or on any other extemporised ground, than while their guest momentarily hung fire; but though he winced it was as if he now liked to wince—the occasions she gave him for doing so were such a sign of his abdication. He had wholly stepped aside, and she could flounder as she would: he had found exactly the formula that saved his dignity, that expressed his sincerity, and that yet didn't touch his curiosity. "I see it would be indelicate for me to go further—yes, love, I do see *that*:" such was the concession he had resorted to for a snap of the particular tension of which we a moment ago took the measure. This had entailed Jane's gravely pronouncing him, for the first time in her life, ridiculous; as if, in common sense—! She used that term also with much freedom now; at the same time that it hadn't prevented her almost immediately asking him if *he* would mind writing her letter. Nothing could suit him more, from the moment she was ostensibly to run the show—as for her benefit he promptly phrased the matter—than that she should involve herself in as many inconsistencies as possible; since if he did such things in spite of his scruple this was as nothing to her needing him at every step in spite of her predominance.

His delicacy was absurd for her because Mora's indecency had made this, by her logic, the only air they could now breathe; yet he knew how it nevertheless took his presence to wind her up to her actual challenge of their guest. Face to face with that personage alone she would have failed of the assurance required for such crudity; deeply unprepared as she really was, poor dear, for the crudity to which she might, as a consequence, have opened the gates. She lived altogether thus—and nothing, to her husband's ironic view, he flattered himself, could be droller—in perpetual yearning, deprecating, in bewildered and muddled communion with the dreadful law of crudity; as if in very truth, to *his* amused sense, the situation hadn't of necessity to be dressed up to the eyes for them in every sort of precaution and paraphrase. Traffle had privately reached the point of seeing it, at its high pitch of mystery and bravery, absolutely defy any common catchword. The one his wife had just employed struck him, while he hunched his shoulders at the ominous pause she had made inevitable for sturdy Puddick, as the vulgarest, and he had time largely to blush before an answer came. He had written, explicitly on Jane's behalf, to request the favour of an interview, but had been careful not to intimate that it was to put that artless question. To have dragged a busy person, a serious person, out from town on the implication of his being treated for reward to so *bete* an appeal—no, one surely couldn't appear to have been concerned in that. Puddick had been under no obligation to come—one might honestly have doubted whether he would even reply. However, his power of reply proved not inconsiderable, as consorted with his having presented himself not a bit ruefully or sulkily, but all easily and coolly, and even to a visible degree in a spirit of unprejudiced curiosity. It was as if he had practically forgotten Traffle's own invasion of him at his studio—in addition to which who indeed knew what mightn't have happened between the Chelsea pair in a distracting or freshly epoch-making way since then?—and was ready to show himself for perfectly good-natured, but for also naturally vague about what they could want of him again. "It depends, ma'am, on the sense I understand you to attach to that word," was in any case the answer to which he at his convenience treated Jane.

"I attach to it the only sense," she returned, "that could force me—by *my* understanding of it—to anything so painful as this inquiry. I mean are you so much lovers as to make it indispensable you should immediately marry?"

"Indispensable to who, ma'am?" was what Traffle heard their companion now promptly enough produce. To which, as it appeared to take her a little aback, he added: "Indispensable to *you*, do you mean, Mrs. Traffle? Of course, you see, I haven't any measure of *that*."

"Should you have any such measure"—and with it she had for her husband the effect now of quite "speaking up"—"if I were to give you my assurance that my niece will come into money when the proper means are taken of making her connection with you a little less—or perhaps I should say altogether less—distressing and irregular?"

The auditor of this exchange rocked noiselessly away from his particular point of dissociation, throwing himself at random upon another, before Mr. Pud-dick appeared again to have made up his mind, or at least to have adjusted his intelligence; but the movement had been on Traffle's part but the instinct to stand off more and more—a vague effort of retreat that didn't prevent the young man's next response to pressure from ringing out in time to overtake him. "Is what you want me to understand then that you'll handsomely pay her if she marries me? Is it to tell me that that you asked me to come?" It was queer, Sidney felt as he held his breath, how he kept liking this inferior person the better—the better for his carrying himself so little like any sort of sneak—on every minute spent in his company. They had brought him there at the very best to patronise him, and now would simply have to reckon with his showing clearly for so much more a person "of the world" than they. Traffic, it was true, was becoming, under the precious initiation opened to him by Mora, whether directly or indirectly, much more a man of the world than ever yet: as much as that at least he could turn over in his secret soul while their visitor pursued. "Perhaps you also mean, ma'am, that you suppose me to require that knowledge to determine my own behaviour—in the sense that if she comes in for money I may clutch at the way to come into it too?" He put this as the straightest of questions; yet he also, it was marked, followed up that side-issue further, as if to fight shy of what Jane wanted most to know. "Is it your idea of me that I haven't married her because she isn't rich enough, and that on what you now tell me I may think better of it? Is that how you see me, Mrs. Traffle?" he asked, at his quiet pitch, without heat.

It might have floored his hostess a little, to her husband's vision, but she seemed at once to sit up, on the contrary, so much straighter, that he, after hearing her, immediately turned round. "Don't you *want*, Mr. Puddick, to be able to marry a creature so beautiful and so clever?"

This was somehow, suddenly, on Jane's part, so prodigious, for art and subtlety, Traffle recognised, that he had come forward again and a remarkable thing had followed. Their guest had noticed his return and now looked up at him from over the tea-table, looked in a manner so direct, so intelligent, so quite amusedly critical, that, afresh, before he knew it, he had treated the little fact as the flicker of a private understanding between them, and had just cynically—for it was scarce covertly—smiled back at him in the independence of it. So there he was again, Sidney Traffle; after having tacitly admitted to Mora that her aunt was a goose of geese—compared to himself and *her*—he was at present putting that young woman's accomplice up to the same view of his conjugal loyalty, which might be straightway reported to the girl. Well, what was he, all the same, to do? Jane *was*, on all the ground that now spread immeasurably about them, a goose of geese: all that had occurred was that she more showily displayed it; and that she might indeed have had a momentary sense of triumph when the best that their friend first found to meet her withal proved still another evasion of the real point. "I don't think, if you'll allow me to say so, Mrs. Traffle, that you've any right to ask me, in respect to Miss Montravers, what I 'want'—or that I'm under any obligation to tell you. I've come to you, quite in the dark, because of Mr. Traffle's letter, and so that you shouldn't have the shadow of anything to complain of. But please remember that I've neither appealed to you in any way nor put myself in a position of responsibility toward you."

So far, but only so far, however, had he successfully proceeded before Jane was down upon him in her new trenchant form. "It's not of your responsibility to us I'm talking, but all of your responsibility to *her*. We efface ourselves," she all effectively bridled, "and we're prepared for every reasonable sacrifice. But we do still a little care what becomes of the child to whom we gave up years of our life. If you care enough for her to live with her, don't you care enough to work out some way of making her your very own by the aid of such help as we're eager to render? Or are we to take from you, as against that, that, even thus with the way made easy, she's so amazingly constituted as to prefer, in the face of the world, your actual terms of intercourse?"

The young man had kept his eyes on her without flinching, and so he continued after she had spoken. He then drank down what remained of his tea and, pushing back his chair, got up. He hadn't the least arrogance, not the least fatuity of type—save so far as it might be offensive in such a place to show a young head modelled as with such an intention of some one of the finer economic uses, and a young face already a little worn as under stress of that economy—but he couldn't help his looking, while he pulled down his not very fresh waistcoat, just a trifle like a person who had expected to be rather better regaled. This came indeed, for his host, to seeing that he looked bored; which was again, for that gentleman, a source of humiliation. What style of conversation, comparatively, on the showing of it, wouldn't he and Mora meanwhile be having together? If they would only invite *him*, their uncle—or rather no, when it came to that, not a bit, worse luck, their uncle—if they would only invite him, their humble admirer, to tea! During which play of reflection and envy, at any rate, Mr. Puddick had prepared to take his leave. "I don't think I can talk to you, really, about my 'terms of intercourse' with any lady." He wasn't superior, exactly—wasn't so in fact at all, but was nevertheless crushing, and all the more that his next word seemed spoken, in its persistent charity, for their help. "If it's important you should get at that sort of thing it strikes me you should do so by the lady herself."

Our friend, at this, no longer stayed his hand. "Mrs. Traffle doesn't see her," he explained to their companion—"as the situation seems to present itself."

"You mean Mora doesn't see me, my dear!" Mrs. Traffle replied with spirit.

He met it, however, with a smile and a gallant inclination. "Perhaps I mean that she only unsuccessfully tries to."

"She doesn't then take the right way!" Mora's aunt tossed off.

Mr. Puddick looked at her blandly. "Then you lose a good deal, ma'am. For if you wish to learn from me how much I admire your niece," he continued straight, "I don't in the least mind answering to that that you may put my sentiments at the highest. I *adore* Miss Montravers," he brought out, after a slight catch of his breath, roundly and impatiently. "I'd do anything in the world for her."

"Then do you pretend," said Jane with a rush, as if to break through this opening before she was checked, "then do you pretend that you're living with her in innocence?"

Sidney Traffle had a groan for it—a hunched groan in which he exhaled the anguish, as he would have called it, of his false position; but Walter Puddick only continued, in his fine unblinking way, to meet Jane's eyes. "I repudiate absolutely your charge of my 'living' with her or of her living with me. Miss Montravers is irreproachable and immaculate."

"All appearances to the contrary notwithstanding?" Mrs. Traffle cried. "You'd do anything in the world for her, and she'd by the same token, I suppose, do anything in the world for you, and yet you ask me to believe that, all the while, you are, together, in this extraordinary way, doing nothing in the world—?" With which, to his further excruciation, her husband, with eyes averted from her, felt her face turn, as for a strained and unnatural intensity of meaning, upon himself. "He attempts, dear, to prove too much! But I only desire," she continued to their guest, "that you should definitely understand how far I'm willing to go."

"It *is* rather far you know," Sidney, at this, in spite of everything, found himself persuasively remarking to Puddick.

It threw his wife straight upon him, and he felt her there, more massively weighted than he had ever known her, while she said: "I'll make it four hundred and fifty. Yes, a year," she then exaltedly pursued to their visitor. "I pass you my word of honour for it. That's what I'll allow Mora as your wife."

Traffle watched him, under this—and the more that an odd spasm or shade had come into his face; which in turn made our friend wish the more to bridge somehow the dark oddity of their difference. What was all the while at bottom sharpest for him was that they might somehow pull more together. "That, you see," he fluted for conciliation, "is her aunt's really, you know, I think, rather magnificent message for her."

The young man took in clearly, during a short silence, the material magnificence—while Traffle again noted how almost any sort of fineness of appreciation could show in his face. "I'm sure I'm much obliged to you," he presently said.

"You don't refuse to let her have it, I suppose?" Mrs. Traffle further proceeded.

Walter Puddick's clear eyes—clear at least as his host had hitherto judged them—seemed for the minute attached to the square, spacious sum. "I don't refuse anything. I'll give her

Henry James

your message."

"Well," said Jane, "that's the assurance we've wanted." And she gathered herself as for relief, on her own side, at his departure.

He lingered but a moment—which was long enough, however, for her husband to see him, as with an in-tenser twinge of the special impatience just noted in him, look, all unhappily, from Mora's aunt to Mora's uncle. "Of course I can't mention to her such a fact. But I wish, all the same," he said with a queer sick smile, "that you'd just simply let us alone."

He turned away with it, but Jane had already gone on. "Well, you certainly seem in sufficient possession of the right way to make us!"

Walter Puddick, picking up his hat and with his distinctly artistic and animated young back presented—though how it came to show so strikingly for such Sidney Traffle couldn't have said—reached one of the doors of the room which was not right for his egress; while Sidney stood divided between the motion of correcting and guiding him and the irresistible need of covering Jane with a last woeful reproach. For he had seen something, had caught it from the sharp flicker of trouble finally breaking through Puddick's face, caught it from the fact that—yes, positively—the upshot of their attack on him was a pair of hot tears in his eyes. They stood for queer, deep things, assuredly, these tears; they spoke portentously, since that was her note, of wonderful Mora; but there was an indelicacy in the pressure that had thus made the source of them public. "You *have* dished us now!" was what, for a Parthian shot, Jane's husband would have liked to leave with her, and what in fact he would have articulately phrased if he hadn't rather given himself to getting their guest with the least discomfort possible out of the room. Into the hall he ushered him, and there—absurd, incoherent person as he had again to know himself for—vaguely yet reassuringly, with an arm about him, patted him on the back. The full force of this victim's original uttered warning came back to him; the probable perfect wisdom of his plea that, since he had infinitely to manage, their line, the aunt's and the uncle's, was just to let him feel his way; the gage of his sincerity as to this being the fact of his attachment. Sidney Traffle seemed somehow to feel the fullest force of both these truths during the moment his young friend recognised the intention of his gesture; and thus for a little, at any rate, while the closed door of the drawing-room and the shelter of the porch kept them unseen and unheard from within, they faced each other for the embarrassment that, as Traffle would have been quite ready to put it, they had in common. Their eyes met their eyes, their conscious grin their grin; hang it, yes, the screw *was* on Mora's lover. Puddick's recognition of his sympathy—well, proved that he needed something, though he didn't need interference from the outside; which couldn't, any way they might arrange it, seem delicate enough. Jane's obtrusion of her four hundred and fifty affected Traffle thus as singularly gross; though part of that association might proceed for him, doubtless, from the remark in which his exasperated sensibility was, the next thing, to culminate.

"I'm afraid I can't explain to you," he first said, however, "why it is that in spite of my indoctrination, my wife fails to see that there's only one answer a gentleman may make to the so intimate question she put to you."

"I don't know anything about that; I wasn't at all making her a conventional reply. But I don't mind assuring you, on my sacred honour—"

So Walter Puddick was going on, but his host, with a firm touch of his arm, and very handsomely, as that host felt, or at least desired to feel, wouldn't have it. "Ah, it's none of my business; I accept what you've said, and it wouldn't matter to you if I didn't. Your situation's evidently remarkable," Traffle all sociably added, "and I don't mind telling you that I, for one, have confidence in your tact. I recognised, that day I went to see you, that this was the only thing to do, and have done my best, ever since, to impress it on Mrs. Traffle. She replies to me that I talk at my ease, and the appearances *are* such, I recognise, that it would be odd she shouldn't mind them. In short she has shown you how much she does mind them. I tell her," our friend pursued, "that we mustn't weigh appearances too much against realities—and that *of* those realities," he added, balancing again a little on his toes and clasping his waist with his hands, which at the same time just worked down the back of his waistcoat, "you must be having your full share." Traffle liked, as the effect of this, to see his visitor look at him harder; he felt how the ideal turn of their relation would be that he should show all the tact he was so incontestably showing, and yet at the same time not miss anything that would be interesting. "You see of course for yourself how little, after all, she knows Mora. She doesn't appreciate the light hand that you must have to have with her—and that, I take it," Sidney Traffle smiled, "is what you contend for with us."

"I don't contend for anything with you, sir," said Walter Puddick.

"Ah, but you do want to be let alone," his friend insisted.

The young man turned graver in proportion to this urbanity. "Mrs. Traffle has closed my mouth."

"By laying on you, you mean, the absolute obligation to

report her offer—?" That lady's representative continued to smile, but then it was that he yet began to see where fine freedom of thought—translated into act at least—would rather grotesquely lodge him. He hung fire, none the less, but for an instant; even though not quite saying what he had been on the point of. "I should like to feel at liberty to put it to you that if, in your place, I felt that a statement of Mrs. Traffle's overture would probably, or even possibly, dish me, I'm not sure I should make a scruple of holding my tongue about it. But of course I see that I can't very well go so far without looking to you as if my motive might be mixed. You might naturally say that I can't *want* my wife's money to go out of the house."

Puddick had an undissimulated pause for the renewed effort to do justice to so much elegant arrangement of the stiff truth of his case; but his intelligence apparently operated, and even to the extent of showing him that his companion really meant, more and more, as well—as well, that is, to *him*—as it was humanly conceivable that Mrs. Traffle's husband *could* mean. "Your difficulty's different from mine, and from the appearance I incur in carrying Miss Montravers her aunt's message as a clear necessity and at any risk."

"You mean that your being conscientious about it may look as if the risk you care least to face is that of not with a little patience coming in yourself for the money?" After which, with a glitter fairly sublime in its profession of his detachment from any stupid course: "You can be sure, you know, that *I'd* be sure—!"

"Sure I'm not a pig?" the young man asked in a manner that made Traffle feel quite possessed at last of his confidence.

"Even if you keep quiet I shall know you're not, and shall believe also you won't have thought me one." To which, in

Henry James

the exaltation produced by this, he next added: "Isn't she, with it all—with all she has done for you I mean—splendidly fond of you?"

The question proved, however, but one of those that seemed condemned to cast, by their action, a chill; which was expressed, on the young man's part, with a certain respectful dryness. "How do you know, sir, what Miss Montravers has done for me?"

Sidney Traffle felt himself enjoy, on this, a choice of replies—one of which indeed would have sprung easiest from his lips. "Oh now, come!" seemed for the instant what he would have liked most to hear himself say; but he renounced the pleasure—even though making up for it a little by his actual first choice. "Don't I know at least that she left the honourable shelter of this house for you?"

Walter Puddick had a wait "I never asked it of her."

"You didn't seduce her, no—and even her aunt doesn't accuse you of it. But that she should have given up—well, what she *has* given up, moderately as you may estimate it," Traffle again smiled—"surely has *something* to say about her case?"

"What has more to say than anything else," Puddick promptly returned to this, "is that she's the very cleverest and most original and most endowed, and in every way most wonderful, person I've known in all my life."

His entertainer fairly glowed, for response, with the light of it. "Thank you then!" Traffle thus radiated.

"'Thank you for nothing!'" cried the other with a short laugh and set into motion down the steps and the garden walk by this final attestation of the essential impenetrability even of an acutest young artist's *vie intime* with a character sketchable in such terms.

Traffle accompanied him to the gate, but wondering, as they went, if it was quite inevitable one should come back to feeling, as the result of every sort of brush with people who were really living, like so very small a boy. No, no, one must stretch to one's tallest again. It restored one's stature a little then that one didn't now mind that this demonstration would prove to Jane, should she be waiting in the drawing-room and watching for one's return, that one had detained their guest for so much privacy in the porch. "Well, take care what you do!" Traffle bravely brought out for good-bye.

"Oh, I shall tell her," Puddick replied under the effect of his renewed pat of the back; and even, standing there an instant, had a further indulgence. "She loathes my unfortunate name of course; but she's such an incalculable creature that my information possibly may fetch her."

There was a final suddenness of candour in it that made Traffle gape. "Oh, our names, and hers—! But is her loathing of yours then all that's the matter?"

Walter Puddick stood some seconds; he might, in pursuance of what had just passed, have been going to say things. But he had decided again the next moment for the fewest possible. "No!" he tossed back as he walked off.

V

"We seem to have got so beautifully used to it," Traffle remarked more than a month later to Jane—"we seem to have lived into it and through it so, and to have suffered and surmounted the worst, that, upon my word, I scarce see what's the matter now, or what, that's so very dreadful, it's doing or has done for us. We haven't the interest of her, no," he had gone on, slowly pacing and revolving things according to his wont, while the sharer of his life, tea being over and the service removed, reclined on a sofa, perfectly still and with her eyes rigidly closed; "we've lost that, and I agree that it was great—I mean the interest of the number of ideas the situation presented us with. That has dropped—by our own act, evidently; we must have simply settled the case, a month ago, in such a way as that we shall have no more acquaintance with it; by which I mean no more of the fun of it. I, for one, confess I miss the fun—put it only at the fun of our having had to wriggle so with shame, or, call it if you like, to live so under arms, against prying questions and the too easy exposure of our false explanations; which only proves, however, that, as I say, the worst that has happened to us appears to be that we're going to find life tame again— as tame as it was before ever Mora came into it so immensely to enrich and agitate it. She has gone out of it, obviously, to leave it flat and forlorn—tasteless after having had for so many months the highest flavour. If, by her not thanking you even though she declines, by her not acknowledging in any way your—as I admit—altogether munificent offer, it seems indicated that we shall hold her to have definitely enrolled herself in the deplorable 'flaunting' class, we must at least recognise that she doesn't flaunt at *us*, at whomever else she may; and that she has in short cut us as neatly and effectively as, in the event of her conclusive, her supreme contumacy, we could have aspired to cut *her*. Never was a scandal, therefore, less scandalous—more naturally a disappointment, that is, to our good friends, whose resentment of this holy calm, this absence of any echo of any convulsion, of any sensation of any kind to be picked up, strikes me as ushering in the only form of ostracism our dissimulated taint, our connection with lurid facts that *might* have gone on making us rather eminently worth while, will have earned for us. But aren't custom and use breaking us in to the sense even of *that* anticlimax, and preparing for us future years of wistful, rueful, regretful thought of the time when everything was nice and dreadful?"

Mrs. Traffle's posture was now, more and more, certainly, this recumbent sightless stillness; which she appeared to have resorted to at first—after the launching, that is, of her ultimatum to Mr. Puddick—as a sign of the intensity with which she awaited results. There had been no results, alas, there were none from week to week; never was the strain of suspense less gratefully crowned; with the drawback, moreover, that they could settle to nothing—not even to the alternative, that of the cold consciousness of slighted magnanimity, in which Jane had assumed beforehand that she should find her last support. Her husband circled about her couch, with his eternal dim whistle, at a discreet distance—as certain as if he turned to catch her in the act that when his back was presented in thoughtful retreat her tightened eyes opened to rest on it with peculiar sharpness. She waited for the proof that she had intervened to advantage—the advantage of Mora's social future—and she had to put up with Sidney's watching her wait. So he, on his side, lived under her tacit criticism of that attention; and had they asked themselves, the comfortless pair—as it's in fact scarce conceivable that they didn't—what it would practically have cost them to receive their niece without questions, they might well have judged their present ordeal much the dearer. When Sidney had felt his wife glare at him undetectedly for a fortnight he knew at least what it meant, and if she had signified how much he might have to pay for it should he presume again to see Mora alone, she was now, in their community of a quietude that had fairly soured on their hands, getting ready to quarrel with him for his poverty of imagination about that menace. Absolutely, the conviction grew for him, she would have liked him better to do something, even something inconsiderate of her to the point of rudeness, than simply parade there in the deference that left her to languish. The fault of this conspicuous propriety, which gave on her nerves, was that it did nothing to refresh their decidedly rather starved sense of their case; so that Traffle was frankly merciless—frankly, that is, for himself— in his application of her warning. There was nothing he would indeed have liked better than to call on Mora—quite, as who should say, in the friendly way to which her own last visit at Wimbledon had set so bright an example. At the same time, though he revelled in his acute reflection as to the partner of his home—"I've only to go, and then come back with some 'new fact,' *a la Dreyfus*, in order to make her sit up in a false flare that will break our insufferable spell"—he was yet determined that the flare, certain to take place sooner or later, should precede his act; so large a licence might he then obviously build upon it. His excursions to town were on occasion, even, in truth, not other than perverse— determined, that is, he was well aware, by their calculated effect on Jane, who could imagine in his absence, each time, that he might be "following something up" (an expression that had in fact once slipped from her), might be having the gumption, in other words, to glean a few straws for their nakeder nest; imagine it, yes, only to feel herself fall back again on the mere thorns of consistency.

It wasn't, nevertheless, that he took all his exercise to this supersubtle tune; the state of his own nerves treated him at moments to larger and looser exactions; which is why, though poor Jane's sofa still remained his centre of radiation, the span of his unrest sometimes embraced half London. He had never been on such fidgety terms with his club, which he could neither not resort to, from his suburb, with an unnatural frequency, nor make, in the event, any coherent use of; so that his suspicion of his not remarkably carrying it off there was confirmed to him, disconcertingly, one morning when his dash townward had been particularly wild, by the free address of a fellow-member prone always to overdoing fellowship and who had doubtless for some time amusedly watched his vague gyrations—"I say, Traff, old man, what in the world, this time, have you got 'on'?" It had never been anything but easy to answer the ass, and was easier than ever now—"'On'? You don't suppose I dress, do you, to come to meet *you?*"—yet the effect of the nasty little mirror of his unsatisfied state so flashed before him was to make him afresh wander wide, if wide half the stretch of Trafalgar Square could be called. He turned into the National Gallery, where the great masters were tantalising more by their indifference than by any offer of company, and where he could take up again his personal tradition of a lawless range. One couldn't be a *raffiné* at Wimbledon—no, not with any comfort; but he quite liked to think how he had never been anything less in the great museum, distinguished as he thus was from those who gaped impartially and did the place by schools. *His* sympathies were special and far-scattered, just as the places of pilgrimage he most fondly reverted to were corners unnoted and cold, where the idol in the numbered shrine sat apart to await him.

So he found himself at the end of five minutes in one of the smaller, one of the Dutch rooms—in a temple bare in very fact at that moment save for just one other of the faithful. This was a young person—visibly young, from the threshold of the place, in spite of the back presented for an instant while a small picture before which she had stopped continued to hold her; but who turned at sound of his entering footfall, and who then again, as by an alertness in this movement, engaged his eyes. With which it was remarkably given to Traffle to feel himself recognise even almost to immediate, to artless extravagance of display, two things; the first that his fellow-votary in the unprofaned place and at the odd morning hour was none other than their invincible Mora, surprised, by this extraordinary fluke, in her invincibility, and the second (oh his certainty of *that!*) that she was expecting to be joined there by no such pale fellow-adventurer as her whilom uncle. It amazed him, as it also annoyed him, on the spot, that his heart, for thirty seconds, should be standing almost still; but he wasn't to be able afterward to blink it that he had at once quite gone to pieces, any slight subsequent success in recovering himself to the contrary notwithstanding. Their happening thus to meet was obviously a wonder—it made him feel unprepared; but what especially did the business for him, he subsequently reflected, was again the renewed degree, and for that matter the developed kind, of importance that the girl's beauty gave her. Dear Jane, at home, as he knew—and as Mora herself probably, for that matter, did—was sunk in the conviction that she was leading a life; but whatever she was doing it was clearly the particular thing she might best be occupied with. How could anything be better for a lovely creature than thus to grow from month to month in loveliness?—so that she was able to stand there before him with no more felt inconvenience than the sense of the mere tribute of his eyes could promptly rectify.

That ministered positively to his weakness—the justice he did on the spot to the rare shade of human felicity, human impunity, human sublimity, call it what one would, surely dwelling in such a consciousness. How could a girl have to think long; have to think more than three-quarters of a second, under any stress whatever, of anything in the world but that her presence was an absolute incomparable value? The prodigious thing, too, was that it had had in the past, and the comparatively recent past that one easily recalled, to content itself with counting twenty times less: a proof precisely that any conditions so determined could only as a matter of course have been odious and, at the last, outrageous to her. Goodness knew with what glare of graceless inaction this rush of recognitions was accompanied in poor Traffle; who was later on to ask himself whether he had showed to less advantage in the freshness of his commotion or in the promptly enough subsequent rage of his coolness. The commotion, in any case, had doubtless appeared more to paralyse than to agitate him, since Mora had had time to come nearer while he showed for helplessly planted. He hadn't even at the moment been proud of his presence of mind, but it was as they afterward haunted his ear that the echoes of what he at first found to say were most odious to him. "I'm glad to take your being here for a sign you've not lost your interest in Art"—that might have passed if he hadn't so almost feverishly floundered on. "I hope you keep up your painting—with such a position as you must be in for serious work; I always thought, you know, that you'd do something if you'd stick to it. In fact we quite miss your not bringing us something to admire as you sometimes did; we haven't, you see, much of an art-atmosphere now. I'm glad you're fond of the Dutch—that little Metsu over there that I think you were looking at is a pet thing of my own; and, if my living to do something myself hadn't been the most idiotic of dreams, something in *his* line—though of course a thousand miles behind him—was what I should have tried to go in for. You see at any rate where—missing as I say our art-atmosphere—I have to come to find one. Not such a bad place certainly"—so he had hysterically gabbled; "especially at this quiet hour—as I see you yourself quite feel. I just turned in—though it does discourage! I hope, however, it hasn't that effect on *you*," he knew himself to grin with the last awkwardness; making it worse the next instant by the gay insinuation: "I'm bound to say it isn't how you look—discouraged!"

It reeked for him with reference even while he said it—for the truth was but too intensely, too insidiously, somehow, that her confidence implied, that it in fact bravely betrayed, grounds. He was to appreciate this wild waver, in retrospect, as positive dizziness in a narrow pass—the abyss being naturally on either side; that abyss of the facts of the girl's existence which he must thus have seemed to rush into, a smirking, a disgusting tribute to them through his excessive wish to show how clear he kept of them. The terrible, the fatal truth was that she made everything too difficult—or that this, at any rate, was how she enjoyed the exquisite privilege of affecting him. She watched him, she saw him splash to keep from sinking, with a pitiless cold sweet irony; she gave him rope as a syren on a headland might have been amused at some bather beyond his depth and unable to swim. It was all the fault—his want of ease was—of the real extravagance of his idea of not letting her spy even the tip of the tail of any "freedom" with her; thanks to which fatality she had indeed the game in her own hands. She exhaled a distinction—it glanced out of every shade of selection, every turn of expression, in her dress, though she had always, for that matter, had the genius of felicity there—which was practically the "new fact" all Wimbledon had been awaiting; and yet so perverse was their relation that to mark at all any special consideration for it was to appear just to make the allusion he was most forbidding himself. It was hard, his troubled consciousness told him, to be able neither to overlook her new facts without brutality nor to recognise them without impertinence; and he was frankly at the end of his resources by the time he ceased beating the air. Then it was, yes, then it was perfectly, as if she had patiently let him show her each of his ways of making a fool of himself; when she still said nothing a moment—and yet still managed to keep him ridiculous—as if for certainty on that head. It was true that when she at last spoke she swept everything away.

"It's a great chance my meeting you—for what you so kindly think of me."

She brought that out as if he had been uttering mere vain sounds—to which she preferred the comparative seriousness of the human, or at least of the mature, state, and her unexpectedness it was that thus a little stiffened him up. "What I think of you? How do you know what I think?"

She dimly and charmingly smiled at him, for it wasn't really that she was harsh. She was but infinitely remote—the syren on her headland dazzlingly in view, yet communicating, precisely, over such an abyss. "Because it's so much more, you mean, than you know yourself? If you don't know yourself, if you know as little as, I confess, you strike me as doing," she, however, at once went on, "I'm more sorry for you than anything else; even though at the best, I dare say, it must seem odd to you to hear me so patronising." It was borne in upon him thus that she would now make no difference, to his honour—to that of his so much more emancipated spirit at least—between her aunt and her uncle; so much should the poor uncle enjoy for his pains. He should stand or fall with fatal Jane—for at this point he was already sure Jane had been fatal; it was in fact with fatal Jane tied as a millstone round his neck that he at present knew himself sinking. "You try to make grabs at some idea, but the simplest never occurs to you."

"What do you call the simplest, Mora?" he at this heard himself whine.

"Why, my being simply a good girl. You gape at it"—he was

trying exactly not to—"as if it passed your belief; but it's really all the while, to my own sense, what has been the matter with me. I mean, you see, a good creature—wanting to live at peace. Everything, however, occurs to you but that—and in spite of my trying to show you. You never understood," she said with her sad, quiet lucidity, "what I came to see you for two months ago." He was on the point of breaking in to declare that the reach of his intelligence at the juncture of which she spoke had been quite beyond expression; but he checked himself in time, as it would strike her but as a vague weak effort to make exactly the distinction that she held cheap. No, he wouldn't give Jane away now— he'd suffer anything instead; the taste of what he should have to suffer was already there on his lips: it came over him, to the strangest effect of desolation, of desolation made certain, that they should have lost Mora for ever, and that this present scant passage must count for them as her form of rupture. Jane had treated her the other day—treated her, that is, through Walter Pud-dick, who would have been, when all was said, a faithful agent—to *their* form, their form save on the condition attached, much too stiff a one, no doubt; so that he was actually having the extraordinary girl's answer. What they thought of her was that she was Walter Puddick's mistress—the only difference between them being that whereas her aunt fixed the character upon her as by the act of tying a neatly inscribed luggage-tag to a bandbox, he himself flourished about with *his* tag in his hand and a portentous grin for what he could do with it if he would. She brushed aside alike, however, vulgar label and bewildered formula; she but took Jane's message as involving an insult, and if she treated him, as a participant, with any shade of humanity, it was indeed that she was the good creature for whom she had a moment ago claimed credit. Even under the sense of so supreme a pang poor Traffle could value his actual, his living, his wonderful impression, rarest treasure of sense, as what the whole history would most have left with him. It was all he should have of her in the future—the mere memory of these dreadful minutes in so noble a place, minutes that were shining easy grace on her part and helpless humiliation on his; wherefore, tragically but instinctively, he gathered in, as for preservation, every grain of the experience. That was it; they had given her, without intending it, still wider wings of freedom; the clue, the excuse, the pretext, whatever she might call it, for shaking off any bond that had still incommoded her. She was spreading her wings—that was what he saw—as if she hovered, rising and rising, like an angel in a vision; it was the picture that he might, if he chose, or mightn't, make Jane, on his return, sit up to. Truths, these, that for our interest in him, or for our grasp of them, press on us in succession, but that within his breast were quick and simultaneous; so that it was virtually without a wait he heard her go on. "Do try—that's really all I want to say—to keep hold of my husband."

"Your husband—?" He *did* gape.

She had the oddest charming surprise—her nearest approach to familiarity. "Walter Puddick. Don't you know I'm married?" And then as for the life of him he still couldn't but stare: "Hasn't he told you?"

"Told us? Why, we haven't seen him—"

"Since the day you so put the case to him? Oh! I should have supposed—!" She would have supposed, obviously, that he might in some way have communicated the fact; but she clearly hadn't so much as assured herself of it. "Then there exactly he is—he doesn't seem, poor dear, to know what to do." And she had on his behalf, apparently, a moment of beautiful anxious, yet at the same time detached and all momentary thought. "That's just then what I mean."

Henry James

"My dear child," Traffle gasped, "what on earth *do* you mean?"

"Well"—and she dropped for an instant comparatively to within his reach—"that it's where you can come in. Where in fact, as I say, I quite wish you would!"

All his wondering attention for a moment hung upon her. "Do you ask me, Mora, to *do* something for you?"

"Yes"—and it was as if no "good creature" had ever been so beautiful, nor any beautiful creature ever so good—"to make him your care. To see that he does get it."

"Get it?" Traffle blankly echoed.

"Why, what you promised him. My aunt's money."

He felt his countenance an exhibition. "She promised it, Mora, to *you*."

"If I married him, yes—because I wasn't fit for her to speak to till I should. But if I'm now proudly Mrs. Puddick—!"

He had already, however, as with an immense revulsion, a long jump, taken her up: "You are, you *are*—?" He gaped at the difference it made and in which then, immensely, they seemed to recover her.

"Before all men—and the Registrar."

"The Registrar?" he again echoed; so that, with another turn of her humour, it made her lift her eyebrows at him.

"You mean it doesn't hold if *that's* the way—?"

"It holds, Mora, I suppose, any way—that makes a real marriage. It is," he hopefully smiled, "real?"

"Could anything be more real," she asked, "than to have become such a thing?"

"Walter Puddick's wife?" He kept his eyes on her pleadingly. "Surely, Mora, it's a *good* thing—clever and charming as he is." Now that Jane had succeeded his instinct, of a sudden, was to back her up.

Mrs. Puddick's face—and the fact was it was strange, in the light of her actual aspect, to think of her and name her so—showed, however, as ready a disposition. "If he's as much as that then why were you so shocked by my relations with him?"

He panted—he cast about. "Why, we didn't doubt of his distinction—of what it was at any rate likely to become."

"You only doubted of mine?" she asked with her harder look.

He threw up helpless arms, he dropped them while he gazed at her. "It doesn't seem to me possible any one can ever have questioned your gift for doing things in your own way. And if you're now married," he added with his return of tentative presumption and his strained smile, "your own way opens out for you, doesn't it? as never yet."

Her eyes, on this, held him a moment, and he couldn't have said now what was in them. "I think it does. I'm seeing," she said—"I shall see. Only"—she hesitated but for an instant—"for that it's necessary you shall look after him."

They stood there face to face on it—during a pause that, lighted by her radiance, gave him time to take from her, somehow, larger and stranger things than either might at all intelligibly or happily have named. "Do you ask it of me?"

"I ask it of you," said Mrs. Puddick after a wait that affected him as giving his contribution to her enjoyment of that title as part of her reason.

He held out, however—contribution or no contribution—another moment. "Do you beg me very hard?"

Once more she hung fire—but she let him have it. "I beg you very hard."

It made him turn pale. "Thank you," he said; and it was as if now he didn't care what monstrous bargain he passed with her—which was fortunate, for that matter, since, when she next spoke, the quantity struck him as looming large.

"I want to be free."

"How can you not?" said Sidney Traffle, feeling, to the most extraordinary tune, at one and the same time both sublime and base; and quite vague, as well as indifferent, as to which character prevailed.

"But I don't want him, you see, to suffer."

Besides the opportunity that this spread before him, he could have blessed her, could have embraced her, for "you see." "Well, I promise you he sha'n't suffer if I can help it."

"Thank you," she said in a manner that gave him, if possible, even greater pleasure yet, showing him as it did, after all, what an honest man she thought him. He even at that point had his apprehension of the queer-ness of the engagement that, as an honest man, he was taking—the engagement, since she so "wanted to be free," to relieve her, so far as he devotedly might, of any care hampering this ideal; but his perception took a tremendous bound as he noticed that their interview had within a moment become exposed to observation. A reflected light in Mora's face, caught from the quarter behind him, suddenly so advised him and caused him to turn, with the consequence of his seeing a gentleman in the doorway by which he had entered—a gentleman in the act of replacing the hat raised to salute Mrs. Puddick and with an accompanying smile still vivid in a clear, fresh, well-featured face. Everything took for Sidney Traffle a sharper sense from this apparition, and he had, even while the fact of the nature of his young friend's business there, the keeping of an agreeable appointment in discreet conditions, stood out for him again as in its odd insolence of serenity and success, the consciousness that whatever his young friend was doing, whatever she was "up to," he was now quite as much in the act of backing her as the gentlemen in the doorway, a slightly mature, but strikingly well-dressed, a pleasantly masterful-looking gentleman, a haunter of the best society, one could be sure, was waiting for him to go. Mora herself, promptly, had that apprehension, and conveyed it to him, the next thing, in words that amounted, with their sweet conclusive look, to a decent dismissal. "Here's what's of *real* importance to me," she seemed to say; "so, though I count on you, I needn't keep you longer." But she took time in fact just to revert. "I've asked him to go to you; and he will, I'm sure, he *will*: by which you'll have your chance, don't fear! Good-bye." She spoke as if this "chance" were what he would now at once be most yearning for; and thus it was that, while he stayed but long enough to let his eyes move again to the new, the impatient and distinctly "smart," yes, unmistakably, this time, not a bit Bohemian candidate for her attention, and then let them come back to herself as for some grasp of the question of a relation already so developed, there might have hung itself up there the prospect of an infinite future of responsibility about Walter Puddick—if only as a make-weight perhaps to the extinction of everything else. When he had turned his back and begun humbly to shuffle, as it seemed to him, through a succession of shining rooms where the walls bristled with eyes that watched him for mockery, his sense was of having seen the last of Mora as completely as if she had just seated herself in the car of a rising balloon that would never descend again to earth.

VI

It was before that aspect of the matter, at any rate, that Sidney Traffle made a retreat which he would have had to regard as the most abject act of his life hadn't he just savingly been able to regard it as the most lucid. The aftertaste of that quality of an intelligence in it sharp even to soreness was to remain with him, intensely, for hours—to the point in fact (which says all) of rendering necessary a thoughtful return to his club rather than a direct invocation of the society of his wife. He ceased, for the rest of the day there, to thresh about; that phase, sensibly, was over for him; he dropped into a deep chair, really exhausted, quite spent, and in this posture yielded to reflections too grave for accessory fidgets. They were so grave, or were at least so interesting, that it was long since he had been for so many hours without thinking of Jane—of whom he didn't even dream after he had at last inevitably, reacting from weeks of tension that were somehow ended for ever, welcomed a deep foodless doze which held him till it was time to order tea. He woke to partake, still meditatively, of that repast—yet, though late the hour and quite exceptional the length of his absence, with his domestic wantonness now all gone and no charm in the thought of how Jane would be worried. He probably shouldn't be wanton, it struck him, ever again in his life; that tap had run dry—had suffered an immense, a conclusive diversion from the particular application of its flow to Jane.

This truth indeed, I must add, proved of minor relevance on his standing before that lady, in the Wimbledon drawing-room, considerably after six o'clock had struck, and feeling himself in presence of revelations prepared not only to match, but absolutely to ignore and override, his own. He hadn't put it to himself that if the pleasure of stretching her on the rack appeared suddenly to have dropped for him this was because "it"—by which he would have meant everything else—was too serious; but *had* he done so he would at once have indulged in the amendment that he himself certainly was. His wife had in any case risen from the rack, the "bed of steel" that, in the form of her habitual, her eternal, her plaintive, aggressive sofa, had positively a pushed-back and relegated air—an air to the meaning of which a tea-service that fairly seemed to sprawl and that even at such an hour still almost unprecedentedly lingered, added the very accent of recent agitations. He hadn't been able not to consult himself a little as to the strength of the dose, or as to the protraction of the series of doses, in which he should administer the squeezed fruit, the expressed and tonic liquor, of his own adventure; but the atmosphere surrounding Jane herself was one in which he felt questions of that order immediately drop. The atmosphere surrounding Jane had been, in fine, on no occasion that he could recall, so perceptibly thick, so abruptly rich, so charged with strange aromas; he could really almost have fancied himself snuff up from it a certain strength of transient tobacco, the trace of a lately permitted cigarette or two at the best—rarest of accidents and strangest of discords in that harmonious whole. Had she, gracious goodness, been smoking with some-body?—a possibility not much less lurid than this conceived extravagance of the tolerated, the independent pipe.

Yes, absolutely, she eyed him through a ranker medium than had ever prevailed between them by any perversity of his; eyed him quite as if prepared, in regular tit-for-tat fashion, to stretch *him*, for a change, on his back, to let him cool his heels in that posture while she sauntered in view pointedly enough for him to tell her how he liked it. Something had happened to her in his absence that made her quite indifferent, in other words, to what might have happened to any one 'else at all; and so little had he to fear asperity on the score of his selfish day off that she didn't even see the advantage to her, for exasperation of his curiosity, of holding him at such preliminary arm's-length as would be represented by a specious "scene." She would have liked him, he easily recognized, to burst with curiosity, or, better still, to grovel with it, before she should so much as throw him a sop; but just this artless pride in her it was that, by the very candour of its extravagance, presently helped him to a keen induction. He had only to ask himself what could have occurred that would most of all things conduce to puffing her up with triumph, and then to reflect that, thoroughly to fill that bill, as who should say, she must have had a contrite call from Mora. He knew indeed, consummately, how superior a resource to morbid contrition that young woman was actually cultivating; in accordance with which the next broadest base for her exclusive command of the situation— and she clearly claimed nothing less—would be the fact that Walter Puddick had been with her and that she had had him (and to the tune of odd revelry withal to which their disordered and unremoved cups glaringly testified) all to herself. Such an interview with him as had so uplifted her that she distractedly had failed to ring for the parlour-maid, with six o'clock ebbing in strides—this did tell a story, Traffle ruefully recognised, with which it might well verily yet be given her to work on him. He was promptly to feel, none the less, how he carried the war across her border, poor superficial thing, when he decided on the direct dash that showed her she had still to count with him.

He didn't offer her, as he looked about, the mere obvious "I see you've had visitors, or a visitor, and have smoked a pipe with them and haven't bored yourself the least mite"—he broke straight into: "He has come out here again then, the wretch, and you've done him more justice? You've done him a good deal, my dear," he laughed in the grace of his advantage, "if you've done him even half as much as he appears to have done your tea-table!" For this the quick flash-light of his imagination—that's what it was for her to have married an imaginative man—was just the drop of a flying-machine into her castle court while she stood on guard at the gate. She gave him a harder look, and he feared he might kindle by too great an ease—as he was far from prematurely wishing to do—her challenge of his own experience. Her flush of presumption turned in fact, for the instant, to such a pathetically pale glare that, before he knew it, conscious of his resources and always coming characteristically round to indulgence as soon as she at all gave way, he again magnanimously abdicated. "He came to say it's no use?" he went on, and from that moment knew himself committed to secrecy. It had tided him over the few seconds of his danger—that of Jane's demanding of him what he had been up to. He didn't want to be asked, no; and his not being asked guarded his not—yes—positively lying; since what most of all now filled his spirit was that he shouldn't himself positively have to speak. His not doing so would be his keeping something all to himself—as Jane would have liked, for the six-and-a-half minutes of her strained, her poor fatuous chance, to keep her passage with Puddick; or to do this, in any case, till he could feel her resist what would certainly soon preponderantly make for her wish to see him stare at her producible plum. It wasn't, moreover, that he could on his own side so fully withstand wonder; the wonder of this new singular ground of sociability between persons hitherto seeing so little with the same eyes. There were things that fitted—fitted somehow the fact of the young man's return, and he could feel in his breastpocket, when it came to that, the presence of the very key to almost any blind or even wild motion, as a sign of trouble, on poor Puddick's part; but what and where was the key to the mystery of Jane's sudden pride in his surely at the best very queer communication? The eagerness of this pride it was, at all events, that after a litde so worked as to enable him to breathe again for his own momentarily menaced treasure. "They're married—they've been married a month; not a bit as one would have wished, or by any form decent people recognise, but with the effect, at least, he tells me, that she's now legally his wife and he legally her husband, so that neither can marry any one else, and that—and that—"

"And that she has taken his horrid name, under our pressure, in exchange for her beautiful one—the one that so fitted her and that we ourselves, when all was said, did like so to keep repeating, in spite of everything, you won't deny, for the pleasant showy thing, compared with our own and most of our friends', it was to have familiarly about?" He took her up with this, as she had faltered a little over the other sources of comfort provided for them by the union so celebrated; in addition to which his ironic speech gained him time for the less candid, and thereby more cynically indulgent, profession of entire surprise. And he immediately added: "They've gone in for the mere civil marriage?"

"She appears to have consented to the very least of one that would do: they looked in somewhere, at some dingy office, jabbered a word or two to a man without h's and with a pen behind his ear, signed their names, and then came out as good as you and me; very much as you and I the other day sent off that little postal-packet to Paris from our grocer's back-shop."

Traffle showed his interest—he took in the news. "Well, you know, you didn't make Church a condition."

"No—fortunately not. I was clever enough," Jane bridled, "for that."

She had more for him, her manner showed—she had that to which the bare fact announced was as nothing; but he saw he must somehow, yes, pay by knowing nothing more than he could catch at by brilliant guesses. That had after an instant become a comfort to him: it would legitimate dissimulation, just as this recognised necessity would make itself quickly felt as the mere unregarded underside of a luxury. "And they're at all events, I take it," he went on, "sufficiently tied to be divorced."

She kept him—but only for a moment. "Quite sufficiently, I gather; and that," she said, "may come."

She made him, with it, quite naturally start. "Are they thinking of it already?"

She looked at him another instant hard, as with the rich expression of greater stores of private knowledge than she could adapt all at once to his intelligence. "You've no conception—not the least.—of how he feels."

Her husband hadn't hereupon, he admitted to himself, all artificially to gape. "Of course I haven't, love." Now that he had decided not to give his own observation away—and this however Puddick might "feel"—he should find it doubtless easy to be affectionate. "But he has been telling *you* all about it?"

"He has been here nearly two hours—as you of course, so far as that went, easily guessed. Nominally—at first—he had come out to see you; but he asked for me on finding you absent, and when I had come in to him seemed to want nothing better—"

"Nothing better than to stay and stay, Jane?" he smiled as he took her up. "Why in the world should he? What I ask myself," Traffle went on, "is simply how in the world you yourself could bear it." She turned away from him, holding him now, she judged, in a state of dependence; she reminded him even of himself, at similar moments of her own *asservissement*, when he turned his back upon her to walk about and keep her unsatisfied; an analogy markedly perceptible on her pausing a moment as under her first impression of the scattered tea-things and then ringing to have them attended to. Their domestic, retarded Rebecca, almost fiercely appeared, and her consequent cold presence in the room and inevitably renewed return to it, by the open door, for several minutes, drew out an interval during which he felt nervous again lest it should occur to his wife to wheel round on him with a question. She did nothing of the sort, fortunately; she was as stuffed with supersessive answers as if she were the latest number of a penny periodical: it was only a matter still of his continuing to pay his penny. She wasn't, moreover, his attention noted, trying to be portentous; she was much rather secretly and perversely serene—the basis of which condition did a little tax his fancy. What on earth had Puddick done to her—since he hadn't been able to bring her out Mora—that had made her distinguishably happier, beneath the mere grimness of her finally scoring at home, than she had been for so many months? The best she could have learned from him—Sidney might even at this point have staked his life upon it—wouldn't have been that she could hope to make Mrs. Puddick the centre of a grand rehabilitative tea-party. "Why then," he went on again, "if they were married a month ago and he was so ready to stay with you two hours, hadn't he come sooner?"

"He didn't come to tell me they were married—not on purpose for that," Jane said after a little and as if the fact itself were scarce more than a trifle—compared at least with others she was possessed of, but that she didn't yet mention.

"Well"—Traffle frankly waited now—"what in the world *did* he come to tell you?"

She made no great haste with it. "His fears."

"What fears—at present?" he disingenuously asked.

"'At present?' Why, it's just 'at present' that he feels he has got to look out." Yes, she was distinctly, she was strangely placid about it. "It's worse to have to have them now that she's his wife, don't you understand?" she pursued as if he were really almost beginning to try her patience. "His difficulties aren't over," she nevertheless condescended further to mention.

She was irritating, decidedly; but he could always make the reflection that if she had been truly appointed to wear him out she would long since have done so. "What difficulties," he accordingly continued, "are you talking about?"

"Those my splendid action—for he grants perfectly that it is and will remain splendid—have caused for him." But her calmness, her positive swagger of complacency over it, *was* indeed amazing.

"Do you mean by your having so forced his hand?" Traffie had now no hesitation in risking.

"By my having forced *hers*," his wife presently returned. "By my glittering bribe, as he calls it."

He saw in a moment how she liked what her visitor had called things; yet it made him, himself, but want more. "She found your bribe so glittering that she couldn't resist it?"

"She couldn't resist it." And Jane sublimely stalked. "She consented to perform the condition attached—as I've mentioned to you—for enjoying it."

Traffle artfully considered. "If she has met you on that arrangement where do the difficulties come in?"

Jane looked at him a moment with wonderful eyes. "For me? They don't come in!" And she again turned her back on him.

It really tempted him to permit himself a certain impatience—which in fact he might have shown hadn't he by this time felt himself more intimately interested in Jane's own evolution than in Mr. Puddick's, or even, for the moment, in Mora's. That interest ministered to his art. "You must tell me at your convenience about yours, that is about your apparently feeling yourself now so beautifully able to sink yours. What I'm asking you about is his—if you've put them so at your ease."

"I haven't put them a bit at their ease!"—and she was at him with it again almost as in a glow of triumph.

He aimed at all possible blankness. "But surely four hundred and fifty more a year—!"

"Four hundred and fifty more is nothing to her."

"Then why the deuce did she marry him for it?—since she apparently couldn't bring herself to without it."

"She didn't marry him that she herself should get my allowance—she married him that he should."

At which Traffle had a bit genuinely to wonder. "It comes at any rate to the same if you pay it to her."

Nothing, it would seem, could possibly have had on Jane's state of mind a happier effect. "I sha'n't pay it to her."

Her husband could again but stare. "You *won't*, dear?" he deprecated.

"I don't," she nobly replied. And then as at last for one of her greater cards: "I pay it to *him*."

"But if he pays it to *her*—?"

"He doesn't. He explains."

Traffle cast about. "Explains—a—to Mora?"

"Explains to me. He *has*," she almost defiantly bridled, "perfectly explained."

Her companion smiled at her. "Ah, *that* then is what took him two hours!" He went on, however, before she could either attenuate or amplify: "It must have taken him that of course to arrange with you—as I understand?—for his monopolising the money?"

She seemed to notify him now that from her high command of the situation she could quite look down on the spiteful sarcastic touch. "We have plenty to arrange. We have plenty to discuss. We shall often—if you want to know—have occasion to meet." After which, "Mora," she quite gloriously brought forth, "hates me worse than ever."

He opened his eyes to their widest. "For settling on her a substantial fortune?"

"For having"—and Jane had positively a cold smile for it—"believed her not respectable."

"Then *was* she?" Traffle gaped.

It did turn on him the tables! "Mr. Puddick continues to swear it." But even though so gracefully patient of him she remained cold.

"You yourself, however, haven't faith?"

"No," said Mrs. Traffle.

"In his word, you mean?"

She had a fine little wait. "In her conduct In his knowledge of it."

Again he had to rise to it. "With other persons?"

"With other persons. Even then."

Traffle thought. "But even when?"

"Even from the first," Jane grandly produced.

"Oh, oh, oh!" he found himself crying with a flush. He had had occasion to colour in the past for her flatness, but never for such an audacity of point. Wonderful, all round, in the light of reflection, seemed what Mora was doing for them. "It won't be her husband, at all events, who has put you up to *that!*"

She took this in as if it might have been roguishly insinuating in respect to her own wit—though not, as who should say, to make any great use of it. "It's what I read—"

"What you 'read'—?" he asked as she a little hung fire.

"Well, into the past that from far back so troubled me. I had plenty to tell *him!*" she surprisingly went on.

"Ah, my dear, to the detriment of his own wife?" our friend broke out.

It earned him, however, but her at once harder and richer look. Clearly she was at a height of satisfaction about something—it spread and spread more before him. "For all that really, you know, she *is* now his wife!"

He threw himself amazedly back. "You mean she practically isn't?" And then as her eyes but appeared to fill it out: "Is that what you've been having from him?—and is that what we've done?"

She looked away a little—she turned off again. "Of course I've wanted the full truth—as to what I've done."

Our friend could imagine that, at strict need; but wondrous to him with it was this air in her as of the birth of a new detachment. "What you've 'done,' it strikes me, might be a little embarrassing for us; but you speak as if you really quite enjoyed it!"

This was a remark, he had to note, by which she wasn't in the least confounded; so that if he had his impression of that odd novelty in her to which allusion has just been made, it might indeed have been quite a new Jane who now looked at him out of her conscious eyes. "He likes to talk to me, poor dear."

She treated his observation as if that quite met it—which couldn't but slightly irritate him; but he hadn't in the least abjured self-control, he was happy to feel, on his returning at once: "And you like to talk with *him*, obviously—since he appears so beautifully and quickly to have brought you round from your view of him as merely low."

She flushed a little at this reminder, but it scarcely pulled her up. "I never thought him low"—she made no more of it than that; "but I admit," she quite boldly smiled, "that I did think him wicked."

"And it's now your opinion that people can be wicked without being low?"

Prodigious really, he found himself make out while she just hesitated, the opinions over the responsibility of which he should yet see her—and all as a consequence of this one afternoon of his ill-inspired absence—ready thus unnaturally to smirk at him. "It depends," she complacently brought out, "on the kind."

"On the kind of wickedness?"

"Yes, perhaps. And"—it didn't at all baffle her—"on the kind of people."

"I see. It's all, my dear, I want to get at—for a proper understanding of the extraordinary somersault you appear to have turned. Puddick has just convinced you that *his* immoralities are the right ones?"

"No, love—nothing will ever convince me that any immoralities deserve that name. But some," she went on, "only seem wrong till they're explained."

"And those are the ones that, as you say, he has been explaining?" Traffle asked with a glittering cheerful patience.

"He has explained a great deal, yes"—Jane bore up under it; "but I think that, by the opportunity for a good talk with him, I've at last understood even more. We weren't, you see, before," she obligingly added, "in his confidence."

"No, indeed," her husband opined, "we could scarcely be said to be. But now we are, and it makes the difference?"

"It makes the difference to *me*," Jane nobly contented herself with claiming. "If I've been remiss, however," she showed herself prepared to pursue, "I must make it up. And doubtless I *have* been."

"'Remiss,'" he stared, "when you're in full enjoyment of my assent to our making such sacrifices for her?"

She gave it, in her superior way, a moment's thought. "I don't mean remiss in act; no, that, thank goodness, we haven't been. But remiss in feeling," she quite unbearably discriminated.

"Ah, that, *par exemple*," he protested, "I deny that I've been for a moment!"

"No"—and she fairly mused at him; "you seemed to have all sorts of ideas; while I," she conceded, "had only one, which, so far as it went, was good. But it didn't go far enough."

He watched her a moment. "I doubtless don't know what idea you mean," he smiled, "but how far does it go now?"

She hadn't, with her preoccupied eyes on him, so much as noticed the ironic ring of it. "Well, you'll see for yourself. I mustn't abandon him."

"Abandon Puddick? Who the deuce then ever said you must?"

"Didn't *you* a little," she blandly inquired, "all the while you were so great on our not 'interfering'?"

"I was great—if great you call it—only," he returned, "so far as I was great for our just a little understanding."

"Well, what I'm telling you is that I think I do at present just a little understand."

"And doesn't it make you feel just a little badly?"

"No"—she serenely shook her head; "for my intention was so good. He does justice now," she explained, "to my intention; or he will very soon—he quite let me see that, and it's why I'm what you call 'happy' With which," she wound up, "there's so much more I can still do. There are bad days, you see, before him—and then he'll have only me. For if she was respectable," Jane proceeded, reverting as imperturbably to their question of a while back, "she's certainly not nice now."

He'd be hanged, Traffle said to himself, if he wouldn't look at her hard. "Do you mean by not coming to thank you?" And then as she but signified by a motion that this she had now made her terms with: "What else then is the matter with her?"

"The matter with her," said Jane on the note of high deliberation and competence, and not without a certain pity for his own want of light, "the matter with her is that she's quite making her preparations, by what he's convinced, for leaving him."

"Leaving him?"—he met it with treasures of surprise.

These were nothing, however, he could feel, to the wealth of authority with which she again gave it out "Leaving him."

"A month after marriage?"

"A month after—their form; and she seems to think it handsome, he says, that she waited the month. *That*," she added, "is what he came above all that we should know."

He took in, our friend, many things in silence; but he presently had his comment. "We've done our job then to an even livelier tune than we could have hoped!"

Again this moral of it all didn't appear to shock her. "He doesn't reproach me," she wonderfully said.

"I'm sure it's very good of him then!" Traffle cried.

But her blandness, her mildness, was proof. "My dear Sidney, Walter *is* very good."

She brought it out as if she had made, quite unaided, the discovery; though even this perhaps was not what he most stared at. "Do you call him Walter?"

"Surely"—and she returned surprise for surprise—"isn't he my nephew?"

Traffle bethought himself. "You recognise the Registrar then for *that*."

She could perfectly smile back. "I don't know that I would if our friend weren't so interesting."

It was quite for Sidney Traffle, at this, as if he hadn't known up to that moment, filled for him with her manner of intimating her reason, what sort of a wife—for coolness and other things—he rejoiced in. Really he had to take time— and to throw himself, while he did so, into pretences. "The Registrar?"

"Don't be a goose, dear!"—she showed she could humour him at last; and it was perhaps the most extraordinary impression he had ever in his life received. "But you'll see," she continued in this spirit. "I mean how I shall interest you." And then as he but seemed to brood at her: "Interest you, I mean, in my interest—for I sha'n't content myself," she beautifully professed, "with your simply not minding it."

"Minding your interest?" he frowned.

"In my poor ravaged, lacerated, pathetic nephew. I shall expect you in some degree to share it."

"Oh, I'll share it if you like, but you must remember how little I'm responsible."

She looked at him abysmally. "No—it *was* mainly me. He brings that home to me, poor dear. Oh, he doesn't scare me!"—she kept it up; "and I don't know that I want him to, for it seems to clear the whole question, and really to ease me a little, that he should put everything before me, his grievance with us, I mean, and that I should know just how he has seen our attitude, or at any rate mine. I was stupid the other day when he came—he saw but a part of it then. It's settled," she further mentioned, "that I shall go to him."

"Go to him—?" Traffle blankly echoed.

"At his studio, dear, you know," Jane promptly supplied. "I want to see his work—for we had some talk about that too. He has made me care for it."

Her companion took these things in—even so many of them as there now seemed to be: they somehow left him, in point of fact, so stranded. "Why not call on *her* at once?"

"That will be useless when she won't receive me. Never, never!" said Jane with a sigh so confessedly superficial that her husband found it peculiarly irritating.

"He has brought *that* 'home' to you?" he consequently almost jibed.

She winced no more, however, than if he had tossed her a flower. "Ah, what he has made me realise is that if he has definitely lost her, as he feels, so we ourselves assuredly have, for ever and a day. But he doesn't mean to lose sight of her, and in that way—"

"In that way?"—Traffle waited.

"Well, I shall always hear whatever there may be. And there's no knowing," she developed as with an open and impartial appetite, "what that mayn't come to."

He turned away—with his own conception of this possible expansive quantity and a sore sense of how the combinations of things were appointed to take place without his aid or presence, how they kept failing to provide for him at all. It was his old irony of fate, which seemed to insist on meeting him at every turn. Mora had testified in the morning to no further use for him than might reside in his making her shuffled-off lover the benevolent business of his life; but even in this cold care, clearly, he was forestalled by a person to whom it would come more naturally. It was by his original and independent measure that the whole case had become interesting and been raised above the level of a mere vulgar scandal; in spite of which he could now stare but at the prospect of exclusion, and of his walking round it, through the coming years—to walk vaguely round and round announcing itself thus at the best as the occupation of his future—in wider and remoter circles. As against this, for warmth, there would nestle in his breast but a prize of memory, the poor little secret of the passage at the Gallery that the day had bequeathed him. He might propose to hug this treasure of consciousness, to make it, by some ingenuity he couldn't yet forecast, his very own; only it was a poor thing in view of their positive privation, and what Jane was getting out of the whole business—*her* ingenuity it struck him he could quite forecast—would certainly be a comparative riot of sympathy. He stood with his hands in his pockets and gazed a little, very sightlessly—that is with an other than ranging vision, even though not other than baffled one too—out of the glimmering square of the window. Then, however, he recalled himself, slightly shook himself, and the next moment had faced about with a fresh dissimulation. "If you talk of her leaving him, and he himself comes in for all your bounty, what then is she going to live upon?"

"On her wits, he thinks and fears; on her beauty, on her audacity. Oh, it's a picture—!" Jane was now quite unshrinkingly able to report from her visitor. Traffle, morally fingering, as it were, the mystic medal under his shirt, was at least equally qualified, on his side, to gloom all yearningly at her; but she had meanwhile testified further to her consistent command of their position. "He believes her to be more than ever—*not* 'respectable.'"

"How, 'more than ever,' if respectable was what she was?"

"It was what she wasn't!" Jane returned.

He had a prodigious shrug—it almost eased him for the moment of half his impatience. "I understood that you told me a moment ago the contrary."

"Then you understood wrong. All I said was that he says she was—but that I don't believe him."

He wondered, following. "Then how does he come to describe her as less so?"

Jane straightened it out—Jane surpassed herself. "He doesn't describe her as less so than she 'was'—I only put her at that. *He*"—oh, she was candid and clear about it!—"simply puts her at less so than she might be. In order, don't you see," she luminously reasoned, "that we shall have it on our conscience that we took the case out of his hands."

"And you allowed to him then that that's how we do have it?"

To this her face lighted as never yet. "Why, it's just the point of what I tell you—that I feel I *must*."

He turned it over. "But why so if you're right?"

She brought up her own shoulders for his density. "I haven't been right. I've been wrong."

He could only glare about. "In holding her then already to have fallen—?"

"Oh dear no, not that! In having let it work me up. Of course I can but take from him now," she elucidated, "what he insists on."

Her husband measured it. "Of course, in other words, you can but believe she was as bad as possible, and yet pretend to him he has persuaded you of the contrary?"

"Exactly, love—so that it shall make us worse. As bad as he wants us," she smiled.

"In order," Traffle said after a moment, "that he may

comfortably take the money?"

She welcomed this gleam. "In order that he may comfortably take it."

He could but gaze at her again. "You *have* arranged it!"

"Certainly I have—and that's why I'm calm. He considers, at any rate," she continued, "that it will probably be Sir Bruce. I mean that she'll leave him for."

"And who in the world is Sir Bruce?"

She consulted her store of impressions. "Sir Bruce Bagley, Bart., I think he said."

Traffle fitted it in silence. "A soldier?" he then asked.

"I'm uncertain—but, as I seem to remember, a patron. He buys pictures."

Traffle could privately imagine it. "And that's how she knows him?"

Jane allowed for his simplicity. "Oh, how she 'knows' people—!"

It still held him, however, an instant. "What sort of a type?"

She seemed to wonder a little at his press of questions, but after just facing it didn't pretend to more than she knew. She was, on this basis of proper relations that she had settled, more and more willing, besides, to oblige. "I'll find out for you."

It came in a tone that made him turn off. "Oh, I don't mind."

With which he was back at the window.

She hovered—she didn't leave him; he felt her there behind him as if she had noted a break in his voice or a moisture in his eyes—a tribute to a natural pang even for a not real niece. He wouldn't renew with her again, and would have been glad now had she quitted him; but there grew for him during the next moments the strange sense that, with what had so bravely happened for her—to the point of the triumph of displaying it to him inclusive—the instinct of compassion worked in her; though whether in respect of the comparative solitude to which her duties to "Walter" would perhaps more or less relegate him, or on the score of his having brought home to him, as she said, so much that was painful, she hadn't yet made up her mind. This, after a little, however, she discreetly did; she decided in the sense of consideration for his nerves. She lingered—he felt her more vaguely about; and in the silence that thus lasted between them he felt also, with its importance, the determination of their life for perhaps a long time to come. He was wishing she'd go—he was wanting not then again to meet her eyes; but still more than either of these things he was asking himself, as from time to time during the previous months he had all subtly and idly asked, what would have been the use, after all, of so much imagination as constantly worked in him. Didn't it let him into more deep holes than it pulled him out of? Didn't it make for him more tight places than it saw him through? Or didn't it at the same time, not less, give him all to himself a life, exquisite, occult, dangerous and sacred, to which everything ministered and which nothing could take away?

He fairly lost himself in that aspect—which it was clear only the vision and the faculty themselves could have hung there, of a sudden, so wantonly, before him; and by the moment attention for nearer things had re-emerged he seemed to know how his wife had interpreted his air of musing melancholy absence. She had dealt with it after her own fashion; had given him a moment longer the benefit of a chance to inquire or appeal afresh; and then, after brushing him good-humouredly, in point of fact quite gaily, with her skirts, after patting and patronising him gently with her finger-tips, very much as he had patted and patronised Walter Puddick that day in the porch, had put him in his place, on the whole matter of the issue of their trouble, or at least had left him in it, by a happy last word. She had judged him more upset, more unable to conclude or articulate, about Mora and Sir Bruce, than she, with her easier power of rebound, had been; and her final wisdom, indeed her final tenderness, would be to show him cheerful and helpful mercy. "No then, I see I mustn't rub it in. You sha'n't be worried. I'll keep it all to myself, dear." With which she would have floated away—with which and some other things he was sensibly, relievingly alone. But he remained staring out at the approach of evening—and it was of the other things he was more and more conscious while the vague grey prospect held him. Even while he had looked askance in the greyness at the importunate fiend of fancy it was riding him again as the very genius of twilight; it played the long reach of its prompt lantern over Sir Bruce Bagley, the patron of promising young lives. He wondered about Sir Bruce, recalling his face and his type and his effect—his effect, so immediate, on Mora; wondered how he had proceeded, how he would still proceed, how far perhaps even they had got by that time. Lord, the fun some people did have! Even Jane, with her conscientious new care—even Jane, unmistakably, was in for such a lot.

Henry James

A ROUND OF VISITS

I

HE had been out but once since his arrival, Mark Monteith; that was the next day after—he had disembarked by night on the previous; then everything had come at once, as he would have said, everything had changed. He had got in on Tuesday; he had spent Wednesday for the most part down town, looking into the dismal subject of his anxiety—the anxiety that, under a sudden decision, had brought him across the unfriendly sea at mid-winter, and it was through information reaching him on Wednesday evening that he had measured his loss, measured above all his pain. These were two distinct things, he felt, and, though both bad, one much worse than the other. It wasn't till the next three days had pretty well ebbed, in fact, that he knew himself for so badly wounded. He had waked up on Thursday morning, so far as he had slept at all, with the sense, together, of a blinding New York blizzard and of a deep sore inward ache. The great white savage storm would have kept him at the best within doors, but his stricken state was by itself quite reason enough.

He so felt the blow indeed, so gasped, before what had happened to him, at the ugliness, the bitterness, and, beyond these things, the sinister strangeness, that, the matter of his dismay little by little detaching and projecting itself, settling there face to face with him as something he must now live with always, he might have been in charge of some horrid alien thing, some violent, scared, unhappy creature whom there was small joy, of a truth, in remaining with, but whose behaviour wouldn't perhaps bring him under notice, nor otherwise compromise him, so long as he should stay to watch it. A young jibbering ape of one of the more formidable sorts, or an ominous infant panther, smuggled into the great gaudy hotel and whom it might yet be important he shouldn't advertise, couldn't have affected him as needing more domestic attention. The great gaudy hotel— The Pocahontas, but carried out largely on "Du Barry" lines—made all about him, beside, behind, below, above, in blocks and tiers and superpositions, a sufficient defensive hugeness; so that, between the massive labyrinth and the New York weather, life in a lighthouse during a gale would scarce have kept him more apart. Even when in the course of that worse Thursday it had occurred to him for vague relief that the odious certified facts couldn't be all his misery, and that, with his throat and a probable temperature, a brush of the epidemic, which was for ever brushing him, accounted for something, even then he couldn't resign himself to bed and broth and dimness, but only circled and prowled the more within his high cage, only watched the more from his tenth story the rage of the elements.

In the afternoon he had a doctor—the caravanserai, which supplied everything in quantities, had one for each group of so many rooms—just in order to be assured that he was *grippe* enough for anything. What his visitor, making light of his attack, perversely told him was that he was, much rather, "blue" enough, and from causes doubtless known to himself—which didn't come to the same thing; but he "gave him something," prescribed him warmth and quiet and broth and courage, and came back the next day as to readminister this last dose. He then pronounced him better, and on Saturday pronounced him well—all the more that the storm had abated and the snow had been dealt with as New York, at a push, knew how to deal with things. Oh, how New York knew how to deal—to deal, that is, with other accumulations lying passive to its hand—was exactly what Mark now ached with his impression of; so that, still threshing about in this consciousness, he had on the Saturday come near to breaking out as to what was the matter with him. The Doctor brought in somehow the air of the hotel—which, cheerfully and conscientiously, by his simple philosophy, the good man wished to diffuse; breathing forth all the echoes of other woes and worries and pointing the honest moral that, especially with such a thermometer, there were enough of these to go round.

Our sufferer, by that time, would have liked to tell some one; extracting, to the last acid strain of it, the full strength of his sorrow, taking it all in as he could only do by himself and with the conditions favourable at least to this, had been his natural first need. But now, he supposed, he *must* be better; there was something of his heart's heaviness he wanted so to give out. He had rummaged forth on the Thursday night half a dozen old photographs stuck into a leather frame, a small show-case that formed part of his usual equipage of travel— he mostly set it up on a table when he stayed anywhere long enough; and in one of the neat gilt-edged squares of this convenient portable array, as familiar as his shaving-glass or the hair-brushes, of backs and monograms now so beautifully toned and wasted, long ago given him by his mother, Phil Blood-good handsomely faced him. Not contemporaneous, and a little faded, but so saying what it said only the more dreadfully, the image seemed to sit there, at an immemorial window, like some long effective and only at last exposed "decoy" of fate. It was *because* he was so beautifully good-looking, because he was so charming and clever and frank—besides being one's third cousin, or whatever it was, one's early schoolfellow and one's later college classmate—that one had abjectly trusted him. To live thus with his unremoved, undestroyed, engaging, treacherous face, had been, as our traveller desired, to live with all of the felt pang; had been to consume it in such a single hot, sore mouthful as would so far as possible dispose of it and leave but cold dregs. Thus, if the Doctor, casting about for pleasantness, had happened to notice him there, salient since he was, and possibly by the same stroke even to know him, as New York—and more or less to its cost now, mightn't one say?—so abundantly and agreeable had, the cup would have overflowed and Monteith, for all he could be sure of the contrary, would have relieved himself positively in tears.

"Oh *he's* what's the matter with me—that, looking after some of my poor dividends, as he for the ten years of my absence had served me by doing, he has simply jockeyed me out of the whole little collection, such as it was, and taken the opportunity of my return, inevitably at last bewildered and uneasy, to 'sail,' ten days ago, for parts unknown and as yet unguessable. It isn't the beastly values themselves, however; that's only awkward and I can still live, though I don't quite know how I shall turn round; it's the horror of *his* having done it, and done it to *me*—without a mitigation or, so to speak, a warning or an excuse." That, at a hint or a jog, is what he would have brought out—only to feel afterward, no doubt, that he had wasted his impulse and profaned even a little his sincerity. The Doctor didn't in the event so much as glance at his cluster of portraits—which fact quite put before our friend the essentially more vivid range of imagery that a pair of eyes transferred from room to room and from one queer case to another, in such a place as that, would mainly be adjusted to. It wasn't for *him* to relieve himself touchingly, strikingly or whatever, to such a man: such a man might much more pertinently—save for professional discretion—have emptied out there his own bag of wonders; prodigies of observation, flowers of oddity, flowers of misery, flowers of the monstrous, gathered in current hotel practice. Countless possibilities, making doctors perfunctory, Mark felt, swarmed and seethed at their doors; it showed for an incalculable world, and at last, on Sunday, he decided to leave his room.

II

Everything, as he passed through the place, went on—all the offices of life, the whole bustle of the market, and withal, surprisingly, scarce less that of the nursery and the playground; the whole sprawl in especial of the great gregarious fireside: it was a complete social scene in itself, on which types might figure and passions rage and plots thicken and dramas develop, without reference to any other sphere, or perhaps even to anything at all outside. The signs of this met him at every turn as he threaded the labyrinth, passing from one extraordinary masquerade of expensive objects, one portentous "period" of decoration, one violent phase of publicity, to another: the heavy heat, the luxuriance, the extravagance, the quantity, the colour, gave the impression of some wondrous tropical forest, where vociferous, bright-eyed, and feathered creatures, of every variety of size and hue, were half smothered between undergrowths of velvet and tapestry and ramifications of marble and bronze. The fauna and the flora startled him alike, and among them his bruised spirit drew in and folded its wings. But he roamed and rested, exploring and in a manner enjoying the vast rankness—in the depth of which he suddenly encountered Mrs. Folliott, whom he had last seen, six months before, in London, and who had spoken to him then, precisely, of Phil Bloodgood, for several years previous her confidential American agent and factotum too, as she might say, but at that time so little in her good books, for the extraordinary things he seemed to be doing, that she was just hurrying home, she had made no scruple of mentioning, to take everything out of his hands.

Mark remembered how uneasy she had made him—how that very talk with her had wound him up to fear, as so acute and intent a little person she affected him; though he had affirmed with all emphasis and flourish his own confidence and defended, to iteration, his old friend. This passage had remained with him for a certain pleasant heat of intimacy, his partner, of the charming appearance, being what she was; he liked to think how they had fraternised over their difference and called each other idiots, or almost, without offence. It was always a link to have scuffled, failing a real scratch, with such a character; and he had at present the flutter of feeling that something of this would abide. *He* hadn't been hurrying home, at the London time, in any case; he was doing nothing then, and had continued to do it; he would want, before showing suspicion—that had been his attitude—to have more, after all, to go upon. Mrs. Folliott also, and with a great actual profession of it, remembered and rejoiced; and, also staying in the house as she was, sat with him, under a spreading palm, in a wondrous rococo salon, surrounded by the pinkest, that is the fleshiest, imitation Boucher panels, and wanted to know if he *now* stood up for his swindler. She would herself have tumbled on a cloud, very passably, in a fleshy Boucher manner, hadn't she been over-dressed for such an exercise; but she was quite realistically aware of what had so naturally happened—she was prompt about Bloodgood's "flight."

She had acted with energy, on getting back—she had saved what she could; which hadn't, however, prevented her losing all disgustedly some ten thousand dollars. She was lovely, lively, friendly, interested, she connected Monteith perfectly with their discussion that day during the water-party on the Thames; but, sitting here with him half an hour, she talked only of her peculiar, her cruel sacrifice—since she should never get a penny back. He had felt himself, on their meeting, quite yearningly reach out to her—so decidedly, by the morning's end, and that of his scattered sombre stations, had he been sated with meaningless contacts, with the sense of people all about him intensely, though harmlessly, animated, yet at the same time raspingly indifferent. *They* would have, he and she at least, their common pang—through which fact, somehow, he should feel less stranded. It wasn't that he wanted to be pitied—he fairly didn't pity himself; he winced, rather, and even to vicarious anguish, as it rose again, for poor shamed Bloodgood's doom-ridden figure. But he wanted, as with a desperate charity, to give some easier turn to the mere ugliness of the main facts; to work off his obsession from them by mixing with it some other blame, some other pity, it scarce mattered what—if it might be some other experience; as an effect of which larger ventilation it would have, after a fashion and for a man of free sensibility, a diluted and less poisonous taste.

By the end of five minutes of Mrs. Folliott, however, he felt his dry lips seal themselves to a makeshift simper. She could *take* nothing—no better, no broader perception of anything than fitted her own small faculty; so that though she must have recalled or imagined that he had still, up to lately, had interests at stake, the rapid result of her egotistical little chatter was to make him wish he might rather have conversed with the French waiter dangling in the long vista that showed the oriental cafe as a climax, or with the policeman, outside, the top of whose helmet peeped above the ledge of a window. She bewailed her wretched money to excess—she who, he was sure, had quantities more; she pawed and tossed her bare bone, with her little extra-ordinarily gemmed and manicured hands, till it acted on his nerves; she rang all the changes on the story, the dire fatality, of her having wavered and muddled, thought of this and but done that, of her stupid failure to have pounced, when she had first meant to, in season. She abused the author of their wrongs—recognising thus too Monteith's right to loathe him—for the desperado he assuredly had proved, but with a vulgarity of analysis and an incapacity for the higher criticism, as her listener felt it to be, which made him determine resentfully, almost grimly, that she shouldn't have the benefit of a grain of *his* vision or *his* version of what had befallen them, and of how, in particular, it had come; and should never dream thereby (though much would she suffer from that!) of how interesting he might have been. She had, in a finer sense, no manners, and to be concerned with her in any retrospect was—since their discourse was of losses—to feel the dignity of history incur the very gravest. It was true that such fantasies, or that any shade of inward irony, would be Greek to Mrs. Folliott. It was also true, however, and not much more strange, when she had presently the comparatively happy thought of "Lunch with *us*, you poor dear!" and mentioned three or four of her "crowd"—a new crowd, rather, for her, all great Sunday lunchers there and immense fun, who would in a moment be turning up—that this seemed to him as easy as anything else; so that after a little, deeper in the jungle and while, under the temperature as of high noon, with the crowd complete and "ordering," he wiped the perspiration from his brow, he felt he was letting himself go. He did that certainly to the extent of leaving far behind any question of Mrs. Folliott's manners. They didn't matter there—nobody's did; and if she ceased to lament her ten thousand it was only because, among higher voices, she couldn't make herself heard. Poor Blood-good didn't have a show, as they might have said, didn't get through at any point; the crowd was so new that—there either having been no hue and cry for him, or having been too many others, for other absconders, in the intervals—they had never so much as heard of him and would have no more of Mrs. Folliott's true inwardness, on that subject at least, than she had lately cared to have of Monteith's.

There was nothing like a crowd, this unfortunate knew, for making one feel lonely, and he felt so increasingly during the meal; but he got thus at least in a measure away from the terrible little lady; after which, and before the end of the hour, he wanted still more to get away from every one else. He was in fact about to perform this manoeuvre when he was checked by the jolly young woman he had been having on his left and who had more to say about the Hotels, up and down the town, than he had ever known a young woman to have to say on any subject at all; she expressed herself in hotel terms exclusively, the names of those establishments playing through her speech as the *leit-motif* might have recurrently flashed and romped through a piece of profane modern music. She wanted to present him to the pretty girl she had brought with her, and who had apparently signified to her that she must do so.

"I think you know my brother-in-law, Mr. Newton Winch," the pretty girl had immediately said; she moved her head and shoulders together, as by a common spring, the effect of a stiff neck or of something loosened in her back hair; but becoming, queerly enough, all the prettier for doing so. He had seen in the papers, her brother-in-law, Mr. Monteith's arrival—Mr. Mark P. Monteith, wasn't it?—and where he was, and she had been with him, three days before, at the time; whereupon he had said "Hullo, what can have brought old Mark back?" He seemed to have believed—Newton had seemed—that that shirker, as he called him, never *would* come; and she guessed that if she had known she was going to meet such a former friend ("Which he claims you are, sir," said the pretty girl) he would have asked her to find out what the trouble could be. But the real satisfaction would just be, she went on, if his former friend would himself go and see him and tell him; he had appeared of late so down.

"Oh, I remember him"—Mark didn't repudiate the friendship, placing him easily; only then he wasn't married and the pretty girl's sister must have come in later: which showed, his not knowing such things, how they had lost touch. The pretty girl was sorry to have to say in return to this that her sister wasn't living—had died two years after marrying; so that Newton was up there in Fiftieth Street alone; where (in explanation of his being "down") he had been shut up for days with bad *grippe*; though now on the mend, or she wouldn't have gone to him, not she, who had had it nineteen times and didn't want to have it again. But the horrid poison just seemed to have entered into poor Newton's soul.

"That's the way it *can* take you, don't you know?" And then as, with her single twist, she just charmingly hunched her eyes at our friend, "Don't you want to go to see him?"

Mark bethought himself: "Well, I'm going to see a lady—"

She took the words from his mouth. "Of course you're going to see a lady—every man in New York is. But Newton isn't a lady, unfortunately for him, to-day; and Sunday afternoon in this place, in this weather, alone—!"

"Yes, isn't it awful?"—he was quite drawn to her.

"Oh, *you've* got your lady!"

"Yes, I've got my lady, thank goodness!" The fervour of which was his sincere tribute to the note he had had on Friday morning from Mrs. Ash, the only thing that had a little tempered his gloom.

"Well then, feel for others. Fit him in. Tell him why!"

"Why I've come back? I'm glad I *have*—since it was to see *you!*" Monteith made brave enough answer, promising to do what he could. He liked the pretty girl, with her straight attack and her free awkwardness—also with her difference from the others through something of a sense and a distinction given her by so clearly having Newton on her mind. Yet it was odd to him, and it showed the lapse of the years, that Winch—as he had known him of old—could *be* to that degree on any one's mind.

III

Outside in the intensity of the cold—it was a jump from the Tropics to the Pole—he felt afresh the force of what he had just been saying; that if it weren't for the fact of Mrs. Ash's good letter of welcome, despatched, characteristically, as soon as she had, like the faithful sufferer in Fiftieth Street, observed his name, in a newspaper, on one of the hotel-lists, he should verily, for want of a connection and an abutment, have scarce dared to face the void and the chill together, but have sneaked back into the jungle and there tried to lose himself. He made, as it was, the opposite effort, resolute to walk, though hovering now and then at vague crossways, radiations of roads to nothing, or taking cold counsel of the long but still sketchy vista, as it struck him, of the northward Avenue, bright and bleak, fresh and harsh, rich and evident somehow, a perspective like a page of florid modern platitudes. He didn't quite know what he had expected for his return—not certainly serenades and deputations; but without Mrs. Ash his mail would have quite lacked geniality, and it was as if Phil Blood-good had gone off not only with so large a slice of his small *peculium*, but with all the broken bits of the past, the loose ends of old relationships, that he had supposed he might pick up again. Well, perhaps he should still pick up a few—by the sweat of his brow; no motion of their own at least, he by this time judged, would send them fluttering into his hand.

Which reflections but quickened his forecast of this charm of the old Paris inveteracy renewed—the so-prized custom of nine years before, when he still believed in results from his fond frequentation of the Beaux Arts; that of walking over the river to the Rue de Marignan, precisely, every Sunday without exception, and sitting at her fireside, and often all offensively, no doubt, outstaying every one. How he had used to want those hours then, and how again, after a little, at present, the Rue de Marignan might have been before him! He had gone to her there at that time with his troubles, such as they were, and they had always worked for her amusement—which had been her happy, her clever way of taking them: she couldn't have done anything better for them in that phase, poor innocent things compared with what they might have been, than be amused by them. Perhaps that was what she would still be—with those of his present hour; now too they might inspire her with the touch she best applied and was most instinctive mistress of: this didn't at all events strike him as what he should most resent. It wasn't as if Mrs. Folliott, to make up for boring him with her own plaint, for example, had had so much as a gleam of conscious diversion over his.

"I'm *so* delighted to see you, I've such immensities to tell you!"—it began with the highest animation twenty minutes later, the very moment he stood there, the sense of the Rue de Marignan in the charming room and in the things about all reconstituted, regrouped, wonderfully preserved, down to the very sitting-places in the same relations, and down to the faint sweet mustiness of generations of cigarettes; but everything else different, and even vaguely alien, and by a measure still other than that of their own stretched interval and of the dear delightful woman's just a little pathetic alteration of face. He had allowed for the nine years, and so, it was to be hoped, had she; but the last thing, otherwise, that would have been touched, he immediately felt, was the quality, the intensity, of her care to see him. She cared, oh so visibly and touchingly and almost radiantly—save for her being, yes, distinctly, a little *more* battered than from even a good nine years' worth; nothing could in fact have perched with so crowning an impatience on the heap of what she had to "tell" as that special shade of revived consciousness of having him in particular to tell it to. It wasn't perhaps much

Henry James

to matter how soon she brought out and caused to ring, as it were, on the little recognised marqueterie table between them (such an anciently envied treasure), the heaviest gold-piece of current history she was to pay him with for having just so felicitously come back: he knew already, without the telling, that intimate domestic tension must lately, within those walls, have reached a climax and that he could serve supremely—oh how he was going to serve!—as the most sympathetic of all pairs of ears.

The whole thing was upon him, in any case, with the minimum of delay: Bob had had it from her, definitely, the first of the week, and it was absolutely final now, that they must set up avowedly separate lives—without horrible "proceedings" of any sort, but with her own situation, her independence, secured to her once for all. She had been coming to it, taking her time, and she had gone through—well, so old a friend would guess enough what; but she was at the point, oh blessedly now, where she meant to stay, he'd see if she didn't; with which, in this wonderful way, he himself had arrived for the cream of it and she was just selfishly glad. Bob had gone to Washington—ostensibly on business, but really to recover breath; she had, speaking vulgarly, knocked the wind out of him and was allowing him time to turn round. Mrs. Folliott moreover, she was sure, would have gone—was certainly believed to have been seen there five days ago; and of course his first necessity, for public use, would be to patch up something with Mrs. Folliott. Mark knew about Mrs. Folliott?—who was only, for that matter, one of a regular "bevy." Not that it signified, however, if he didn't: she would tell him about *her* later.

He took occasion from the first fraction of a break not quite to know what he knew about Mrs. Folliott—though perhaps he could imagine a little; and it was probably at this minute that, having definitely settled to a position, and precisely in his very own tapestry *bergere*, the one with the delicious little spectral "subjects" on the back and seat, he partly exhaled, and yet managed partly to keep to himself, the deep resigned sigh of a general comprehension. He knew what he was "in" for, he heard her go on—she said it again and again, seemed constantly to be saying it while she smiled at him with her peculiar fine charm, her positive gaiety of sensibility, scarce dimmed: "I'm just selfishly glad, just selfishly glad!" Well, she was going to have reason to be; she was going to put the whole case to him, all her troubles and plans, and each act of the tragi-comedy of her recent existence, as to the dearest and safest sympathiser in all the world. There would be no chance for *his* case, though it was so much for his case he had come; yet there took place within him but a mild, dumb convulsion, the momentary strain of his substituting, by the turn of a hand, one prospect of interest for another.

Squaring himself in his old *bergere*, and with his lips, during the effort, compressed to the same passive grimace that had an hour or two before operated for the encouragement of Mrs. Folliott—just as it was to clear the stage completely for the present more prolonged performance—he shut straight down, as he even in the act called it to himself, on any personal claim for social consideration and rendered a perfect little agony of justice to the grounds of his friend's vividness. For it was all the justice that could be expected of him that, though, secretly, he wasn't going to be interested in her being interesting, she was yet going to be so, all the same, by the very force of her lovely material (Bob Ash *was* such a pure pearl of a donkey!) and he was going to keep on knowing she was—yes, to the very end. When after the lapse of an hour he rose to go, the rich fact that she *had* been was there between them, and with an effect of the frankly, fearlessly, harmlessly intimate fireside passage for it that went beyond even the best memories of the pleasant past. He hadn't "amused" her, no, in quite the same way as in the Rue de Marignan time—it had then been he who for the most part took frequent turns, emphatic, explosive, elocutionary, over that wonderful waxed parquet while she laughed as for the young perversity of him from the depths of the second, the matching *bergere*. To-day she herself held and swept the floor, putting him merely to the trouble of his perpetual "Brava!" But that was all through the change of basis—the amusement, another name only for the thrilled absorption, having been inevitably for *him*; as how could it have failed to be with such a regular "treat" to his curiosity? With the tea-hour now other callers were turning up, and he got away on the plea of his wanting so to think it all over. He hoped again he hadn't too queer a grin with his assurance to her, as if she would quite know what he meant, that he had been thrilled to the core. But she returned, quite radiantly, that he had carried *her* completely away; and her sincerity was proved by the final frankness of their temporary parting. "My pleasure of you is selfish, horribly, I admit; so that if *that* doesn't suit you—!" Her faded beauty flushed again as she said it.

IV

In the street again, as he resumed his walk, he saw how perfectly it would *have* to suit him and how he probably for a long time wouldn't be suited otherwise. Between them and that time, however, what mightn't, for him, poor devil, on his new basis, have happened? She wasn't at any rate within any calculable period going to care so much for anything as for the so quaintly droll terms in which her rearrangement with her husband—thanks to that gentleman's inimitable fatuity—would have to be made. This was what it was to own, exactly, her special grace—the brightest gaiety in the finest sensibility; *such* a display of which combination, Mark felt as he went (if he could but have done it still more justice) she must have regaled him with! That exquisite last flush of her fadedness could only remain with him; yet while he presently stopped at a street-corner in a district redeemed from desolation but by the passage just then of a choked trolley-car that howled, as he paused for it, beneath the weight of its human accretions, he seemed to know the inward "sinking" that had been determined in a hungry man by some extravagant sight of the preparation of somebody else's dinner. Florence Ash was dining, so to speak, off the feast of appreciation, appreciation of what she had to "tell" him, that he had left her seated at; and she was welcome, assuredly—welcome, welcome, welcome, he musingly, he wistfully, and yet at the same time a trifle mechanically, repeated, stayed as he was a moment longer by the suffering shriek of another public vehicle and a sudden odd automatic return of his mind to the pretty girl, the flower of Mrs. Folliott's crowd, who had spoken to him of Newton Winch. It was extraordinarily as if, on the instant, she reminded him, from across the town, that she had offered him dinner: it was really quite strangely, while he stood there, as if she had told him where he could go and get it. With which, none the less,

Henry James

it was apparently where he wouldn't find her—and what was there, after all, of nutritive in the image of Newton Winch? He made up his mind in a moment that it owed that property, which the pretty girl had somehow made imputable, to the fact of its simply being just then the one image of anything known to him that the terrible place had to offer. Nothing, he a minute later reflected, could have been so "rum" as that, sick and sore, of a bleak New York eventide, he should have had nowhere to turn if not to the said Fiftieth Street.

That was the direction he accordingly took, for when he found the number given him by the same remarkable agent of fate also present to his memory he recognised the direct intervention of Providence and how it absolutely required a miracle to explain his so precipitately embracing this loosest of connections. The miracle indeed soon grew clearer: Providence had, on some obscure system, chosen this very ridiculous hour to save him from cultivation of the sin of selfishness, the obsession of egotism, and was breaking him to its will by constantly directing his attention to the claims of others. Who could say what at that critical moment mightn't have become of Mrs. Folliott (otherwise too then so sadly embroiled!) if she hadn't been enabled to air to him her grievance and her rage?—just as who could deny that it must have done Florence Ash a world of good to have put her thoughts about Bob in order by the aid of a person to whom the vision of Bob in the light of those thoughts (or in other words to whom *her* vision of Bob and nothing else) would mean so delightfully much? It was on the same general lines that poor Newton Winch, bereft, alone, ill, perhaps dying, and with the drawback of a not very sympathetic perso- nality—as Mark remembered it at least—to contend against in almost any conceivable appeal to human furtherance, it was on these lines, very much, that the luckless case in Fiftieth Street was offered him as a source of salutary discipline. The moment for such a lesson might strike him as strange, in view of the quite special and independent opportunity for exercise that his spirit had during the last three days enjoyed there in his hotel bedroom; but evidently his languor of charity needed some admonition finer than any it might trust to chance for, and by the time he at last, Winch's residence recognised, was duly elevated to his level and had pressed the electric button at his door, he felt himself acting indeed as under stimulus of a sharp poke in the side.

V

Within the apartment to which he had been admitted, moreover, the fine intelligence we have imputed to him was in the course of three minutes confirmed; since it took him no longer than that to say to himself, facing his old acquaintance, that he had never seen any one so improved. The place, which had the semblance of a high studio light as well as a general air of other profusions and amplitudes, might have put him off a little by its several rather glaringly false accents, those of contemporary domestic "art" striking a little wild. The scene was smaller, but the rich confused complexion of the Pocahontas, showing through Du Barry paint and patches, might have set the example—which had been followed with the costliest candour—so that, clearly, Winch was in these days rich, as most people in New York seemed rich; as, in spite of Bob's depredations, Florence Ash was, as even Mrs. Folliott was in spite of Phil Bloodgood's, as even Phil Bloodgood himself must have been for reasons too obvious; as in fine every one had a secret for being, or for feeling, or for looking, every one at least but Mark Monteith.

These facts were as nothing, however, in presence of his quick and strong impression that his pale, nervous, smiling, clean-shaven host had undergone since their last meeting some extraordinary process of refinement. He had been ill, unmistakably, and the effects of a plunge into plain clean living, where any fineness had remained, were often startling, sometimes almost charming. But independently of this, and for a much longer time, some principle of intelligence, some art of life, would discernibly have worked in him. Remembered from college years and from those two or three luckless and faithless ones of the Law School as constitutionally common, as consistently and thereby doubtless even rather powerfully coarse, clever only for uncouth and questionable things, he yet presented himself now as if he had suddenly and mysteriously been educated. There was a charm in his wide, "drawn," convalescent smile, in the way his fine fingers—had he anything like fine fingers of old?—played, and just fidgeted, over the prompt and perhaps a trifle incoherent offer of cigars, cordials, ashtrays, over the question of his visitor's hat, stick, fur coat, general best accommodation and ease; and how the deuce, accordingly, had charm, for coming out so on top, Mark wondered, "squared" the other old elements? For the short interval so to have dealt with him what force had it turned on, what patented process, of the portentous New York order in which there were so many, had it skilfully applied? Were these the things New York did when you just gave her all her head, and that he himself then had perhaps too complacently missed? Strange almost to the point of putting him positively off at first—quite as an exhibition of the uncanny—this sense of Newton's having all the while neither missed nor muffed anything, and having, as with an eye to the *coup de theatre* to come, lowered one's expectations, at the start, to that abject pitch. It might have been taken verily for an act of bad faith—really for such a rare stroke of subtlety as could scarce have been achieved by a straight or natural aim.

So much as this at least came and went in Monteith's agitated mind; the oddest intensity of apprehension, admiration, mystification, which the high north-light of the March afternoon and the quite splendidly vulgar appeal of fifty overdone decorative effects somehow fostered and sharpened. Everything had already gone, however, the next moment, for wasn't the man he had come so much too intelligently himself to patronise absolutely bowling him over with the extraordinary speech: "See here, you know— you must be ill, or have had a bad shock, or some beastly upset: are you very sure you ought to have come out?" Yes, he after an instant believed his ears; coarse common Newton Winch, whom he had called on because he could, as a gentleman, after all afford to, coarse common Newton Winch, who had had troubles and been epidemically poisoned, lamentably sick, who bore in his face and in the very tension, quite exactly the "charm," of his manner, the traces of his late ordeal, and, for that matter, of scarce completed gallant emergence—this astonishing ex-comrade was simply writing himself at a stroke (into our friend's excited imagination at all events) the most distinguished of men. Oh, *he* was going to be interesting, if Florence Ash had been going to be; but Mark felt how, under the law of a lively present difference, that would be as an effect of one's having one's self thoroughly rallied. He knew within the minute that the tears stood in his eyes; he stared through them at his friend with a sharp "Why, how do you know? How *can* you?" To which he added before Winch could speak: "I met your charming sister-in-law a couple of hours since—at luncheon, at the Pocahontas; and heard from her that you were badly laid up and had spoken of me. So I came to minister to you."

The object of this design hovered there again, considerably restless, shifting from foot to foot, changing his place, beginning and giving up motions, striking matches for a fresh cigarette, offering them again, redundantly, to his guest and then not lighting himself—but all the while with the smile of another creature than the creature known to Mark; all the while with the history of something that had happened to him ever so handsomely shining out. Mark was conscious within himself from this time on of two quite distinct processes of notation—that of his practically instant surrender to the consequences of the act of perception in his host of which the two women trained suppos-ably in the art of pleasing had been altogether incapable; and that of some other condition on Newton's part that left his own poor power of divination nothing less than shamed. This last was signally the case on the former's saying, ever so respon- sively, almost radiantly, in answer to his account of how he happened to come: "Oh then it's very interesting!" *That* was the astonishing note, after what he had been through: neither Mrs. Folliott nor Florence Ash had so much as hinted or breathed to him that *he* might have incurred that praise. No wonder therefore he was now taken—with this fresh party's instant suspicion and imputation of it; though it was indeed for some minutes next as if each tried to see which could accuse the other of the greater miracle of penetration. Mark was so struck, in a word, with the extraordinarily straight guess Winch had had there in reserve for him that, other quick impressions helping, there was nothing for him but to bring out, himself: "There must be, my dear man, something rather wonderful the matter with you!" The quite more intensely and more irresistibly drawn grin, the quite unmistakably deeper consciousness in the dark, wide eye, that accompanied the not quite immediate answer to which remark he was afterward to remember. "How do you know that—or why do you think it?" "Because there *must* be—for you to see! I shouldn't have expected it."

"Then you take me for a damned fool?" laughed wonderful Newton Winch.

VI

He could say nothing that, whether as to the sense of it or as to the way of it, didn't so enrich Mark's vision of him that our friend, after a little, as this effect proceeded, caught himself in the act of almost too curiously gaping. Everything, from moment to moment, fed his curiosity; such a question, for instance, as whether the quite ordinary peepers of the Newton Winch of their earlier youth could have looked, under any provocation, either dark or wide; such a question, above all, as how *this* incalculable apparition came by the whole startling power of play of its extravagantly sensitive labial connections—exposed, so to its advantage (he now jumped at one explanation) by the removal of what had probably been one of the vulgar-est of moustaches. With this, at the same time, the oddity of that particular consequence was vivid to him; the glare of his curiosity fairly lasting while he remembered how he had once noted the very opposite turn of the experiment for Phil Bloodgood. He would have said in advance that poor Winch couldn't have afforded to risk showing his "real" mouth; just as he would have said that in spite of the fine ornament that so considerably muffled it Phil could only have gained by showing his. But to have seen Phil shorn—as he once had done—was earnestly to pray that he might promptly again bristle; beneath Phil's moustache lurked nothing to "make up" for it in case of removal. While he thought of which things the line of grimace, as he could only have called it, the mobile, interesting, ironic line the great double curve of which connected, in the face before him, the strong nostril with the lower cheek, became the very key to his first idea of Newton's capture of refinement. He had shaved and was happily transfigured. Phil Bloodgood had shaved and been wellnigh lost; though why should he just now too precipitately drag the reminiscence in?

That question too, at the queer touch of association, played up for Mark even under so much proof that the state of his own soul was being with the lapse of every instant registered. Phil Bloodgood had brought about the state of his soul—there was accordingly that amount of connection; only it became further remarkable that from the moment his companion had sounded him, and sounded him, he knew, down to the last truth of things, his disposition, his necessity to talk, the desire that had in the morning broken the spell of his confinement, the impulse that had thrown him so defeatedly into Mrs. Folliott's arms and into Florence Ash's, these forces seemed to feel their impatience ebb and their discretion suddenly grow. His companion was talking again, but just then, incongruously, made his need to communicate lose itself. It was as if his personal case had already been touched by some tender hand—and that, after all, was the modest limit of its greed. "I know now why you came back—did Lottie mention how I had wondered? But sit down, sit down—only let me, nervous beast as I am, take it standing!—and believe me when I tell you that I've now ceased to wonder. My dear chap, I *have* it! It can't but have been for poor Phil Blood-good. He sticks out of you, the brute—as how, with what he has done to you, shouldn't he? There was a man to see me yesterday—Tim Slater, whom I don't think you know, but who's 'on' everything within about two minutes of its happening (I never saw such a fellow!) and who confirmed my supposition, all my own, however, mind you, at first, that you're one of the sufferers. So how the devil can you *not* feel knocked? Why *should* you look as if you were having the time of your life? What a hog to have played it on *you*, on *you*, of all his friends!" So Newton Winch continued, and so the air between the two men might have been, for a momentary watcher—which is indeed what I can but invite the reader to become—that of a nervously displayed, but all considerate, as well as most acute, curiosity on the one side, and that on the other, after a little, of an eventually fascinated acceptance of so much free and in especial of so much right attention. "Do you *mind* my asking you? Because if you do I won't press; but as a man whose own responsibilities, some of 'em at least, don't differ much, I gather, from some of his, one would like to know how he was ever allowed to get to the point—! But I *do* plough you up?"

Mark sat back in his chair, moved but holding himself, his elbows squared on each arm, his hands a bit convulsively interlocked across him—very much in fact as he had appeared an hour ago in the old tapestry *bergere*; but as his rigour was all then that of the grinding effort to profess and to give, so it was considerably now for the fear of too hysterically gushing. Somehow too—since his wound was to that extent open—he winced at hearing the author of it branded. He hadn't so much minded the epithets Mrs. Folliott had applied, for they were to the appropriator of *her* securities. As the appropriator of his own he didn't so much want to brand him as—just more "amusingly" even, if one would.—to make out, perhaps, with intelligent help, how such a man, in such a relation, *could* come to tread such a path: which was exactly the interesting light that Winch's curiosity and sympathy were there to assist him to. He pleaded at any rate immediately his advertising no grievance. "I feel sore, I admit, and it's a horrid sort of thing to have had happen; but when you call him a brute and a hog I rather squirm, for brutes and hogs never live, I guess, in the sort of hell in which he now must be."

Newton Winch, before the fireplace, his hands deep in his pockets, where his guest could see his long fingers beat a tattoo on his thighs, Newton Winch dangled and swung himself, and threw back his head and laughed. "Well, I must say you take it amazingly!—all the more that to see you again this way is to feel that if, all along, there was a man whose delicacy and confidence and general attitude might have marked him for a particular consideration, you'd have been the man." And they were more directly face to face again; with Newton smiling and smiling *so* appreciatively; making our friend in fact almost ask himself when before a man had ever grinned from ear to ear to the effect of its so becoming him. What he replied, however, was that Newton described in those flattering terms a client temptingly fatuous; after which, and the exchange of another protest or two in the interest of justice and decency, and another plea or two in that of the still finer contention that even the basest misdeeds had always somewhere or other, could one get at it, their propitiatory side, our hero found himself on his feet again, under the influence of a sudden failure of everything but horror—a horror determined by some turn of their talk and indeed by the very fact of the freedom of it. It was as if a far-borne sound of the hue and cry, a vision of his old friend hunted and at bay, had suddenly broken in—this other friend's, this irresistibly intelligent other companion's, practically vivid projection of that making the worst ugliness real. "Oh, it's just making my wry face to somebody, and your letting me and caring and wanting to know: that," Mark said, "is what does me good; not any other hideous question. I mean I don't take any interest in *my* case—what one wonders about, you see, is what can be done for him. I mean, that is"—for he floundered a little, not knowing at last quite what he did mean, a great rush of mere memories, a great humming sound as of thick, thick echoes, rising now to an assault that he met with his face indeed contorted. If he didn't take care he should howl; so he more or less successfully took care—yet with his host vividly watching him while he shook the danger temporarily off. "I don't mind—though it's rather *that*; my having felt this morning, after three dismal dumb bad days, that one's friends perhaps would be thinking of one. All I'm conscious of now—I give you my word—is that I'd like to see him."

"You'd like to see him?"

"Oh, I don't say," Mark ruefully smiled, "that I should like him to see *me*—!"

Newton Winch, from where he stood—and they were together now, on the great hearth-rug that was a triumph of modern orientalism—put out one of the noted fine hands and, with an expressive headshake, laid it on his shoulder. "Don't wish him that, Monteith—don't wish him that!"

"Well, but,"—and Mark raised his eyebrows still higher— "he'd see I bear up; pretty well!"

"God forbid he should see, my dear fellow!" Newton cried as for the pang of it.

Mark had for his idea, at any rate, the oddest sense of an exaltation that grew by this use of frankness. "I'd go to him. Hanged if I wouldn't—anywhere!"

His companion's hand still rested on him. "You'd go to him?"

Mark stood up to it—though trying to sink solemnity as pretentious. "I'd go like a shot." And then he added: "And it's probably what—when we've turned round—I *shall* do."

"When 'we' have turned round?"

"Well"—he was a trifle disconcerted at the tone—"I say that because you'll have helped me."

"Oh, I do nothing but want to help you!" Winch replied— which made it right again; especially as our friend still felt himself reassuringly and sustainingly grasped. But Winch went on: "You *would* go to him—in kindness?"

"Well—to understand."

"To understand how he could swindle you?"

"Well," Mark kept on, "to try and make out with him how, after such things—!" But he stopped; he couldn't name them.

It was as if his companion knew. "Such things as you've done for him of course—such services as you've rendered him."

"Ah, from far back. If I could tell you," our friend vainly wailed—"if I could tell you!"

Newton Winch patted his shoulder. "Tell me—tell me!"

"The sort of relation, I mean; ever so many things of a kind—!" Again, however, he pulled up; he felt the tremor of his voice.

"Tell me, tell me," Winch repeated with the same movement.

The tone in it now made their eyes meet again, and with this presentation of the altered face Mark measured as not before, for some reason, the extent of the recent ravage. "You must have been ill indeed."

"Pretty bad. But I'm better. And you do me good"—with which the light of convalescence came back.

"I don't awfully bore you?"

Winch shook his head. "You keep me up—and you see how no one else comes near me."

Mark's eyes made out that he was better—though it wasn't

yet that nothing was the matter with him. If there was ever a man with whom there was still something the matter—! Yet one couldn't insist on that, and meanwhile he clearly did want company. "Then there we are. I myself had no one to go to."

"You save my life," Newton renewedly grinned.

VII

"Well, it's your own fault," Mark replied to that, "if you make me take advantage of you." Winch had withdrawn his hand, which was back, violently shaking keys or money, in his trousers pocket; and in this position he had abruptly a pause, a sensible, absence, that might have represented either some odd drop of attention, some turn-off to another thought, or just simply the sudden act of listening. His guest had indeed himself—under suggestion—the impression of a sound. "Mayn't you perhaps—if you hear something—have a call?"

Mark had said it so lightly, however, that he was the more struck with his host's appearing to turn just paler; and, with it, the latter now *was* listening. "You hear something?"

"I thought *you* did." Winch himself, on Mark's own pressure of the outside bell, had opened the door of the apartment—an indication then, it sufficiently appeared, that Sunday afternoons were servants', or attendants', or even trained nurses' holidays. It had also marked the stage of his convalescence, and to that extent—after his first flush of surprise—had but smoothed Monteith's way. At present he barely gave further attention; detaching himself as under some odd cross-impulse, he had quitted the spot and then taken, in the wide room, a restless turn—only, however, to revert in a moment to his friend's just-uttered deprecation of the danger of boring him. "If I make you take advantage of me—that is blessedly talk to me—it's exactly what I want to do. Talk to me—talk to me!" He positively waved it on; pulling up again, however, in his own talk, to say with a certain urgency: "Hadn't you better sit down?"

Mark, who stayed before the fire, couldn't but excuse

himself. "Thanks—I'm very well so. I think of things and I fidget."

Winch stood a moment with his eyes on the ground. "Are you very sure?"

"Quite—I'm all right if you don't mind."

"Then as you like!" With which, shaking to extravagance again his long legs, Newton had swung off—only with a movement that, now his back was turned, affected his visitor as the most whimsical of all the forms of his rather unnatural manner. He was curiously different with his back turned, as Mark now for the first time saw it—dangling and somewhat wavering, as from an excess of uncertainty of gait; and this impression was so strange, it created in our friend, uneasily and on the spot, such a need of explanation, that his speech was stayed long enough to give Winch time to turn round again. The latter had indeed by this moment reached one of the limits of the place, the wide studio bay, where he paused, his back to the light and his face afresh presented, to let his just passingly depressed and quickened eyes take in as much as possible of the large floor, range over it with such brief freedom of search as the disposition of the furniture permitted. He was looking for something, though the betrayed reach of vision was but of an instant. Mark caught it, however, and with his own sensibility all in vibration, found himself feeling at once that it meant something and that what it meant was connected with his entertainer's slightly marked appeal to him, the appeal of a moment before, not to remain standing. Winch knew by this time quite easily enough that he was hanging fire; which meant that they were suddenly facing each other across the wide space with a new consciousness.

Everything had changed—changed extraordinarily with the

mere turning of that gentleman's back, the treacherous aspect of which its owner couldn't surely have suspected. If the question was of the pitch of their sensibility, at all events, it wouldn't be Mark's that should vibrate to least purpose. Visibly it had come to his host that something had within the few instants remarkably happened, but there glimmered on him an induction that still made him keep his own manner. Newton himself might now resort to any manner he liked. His eyes had raked the floor to recover the position of something dropped or misplaced, and something, above all, awkward or compromising; and he had wanted his companion not to command this scene from the hearth-rug, the hearthrug where he had been just before holding him, hypnotising him to blindness, *because* the object in question would there be most exposed to sight Mark embraced this with a further drop—while the apprehension penetrated—of his power to go on, and with an immense desire at the same time that his eyes should seem only to look at his friend; who broke out now, for that matter, with a fresh appeal. "Aren't you going to take advantage of me, man—aren't you going to *take* it?"

Everything had changed, we have noted, and nothing could more have proved it than the fact that, by the same turn, sincerity of desire had dropped out of Winch's chords, while irritation, sharp and almost imperious, had come in. "That's because he sees I see something!" Mark said to himself; but he had no need to add that it shouldn't prevent his seeing more—for the simple reason that, in a miraculous fashion, this was exactly what he did do in glaring out the harder. It was beyond explanation, but the very act of blinking thus in an attempt at showy steadiness became one and the same thing with an optical excursion lasting the millionth of a minute and making him aware that the edge of a rug, at the point where an arm-chair, pushed a little out of position, over-straddled it, happened just not wholly to have covered in something small and queer, neat and bright, crooked and compact, in spite of the strong toe-tip surreptitiously applied to giving it the right lift Our gentleman, from where he hovered, and while looking straight at the master of the scene, yet saw, as by the tiny flash of a reflection from fine metal, *under* the chair. What he recognised, or at least guessed at, as sinister, made him for a moment turn cold, and that chill was on him while Winch again addressed him—as differently as possible from any manner yet used. "I beg of you in God's name to talk to me—to *talk* to me!"

It had the ring of pure alarm and anguish, but was by this turn at least more human than the dazzling glitter of intelligence to which the poor man had up to now been treating him. "It's you, my good friend, who are in deep trouble," Mark was accordingly quick to reply, "and I ask your pardon for being so taken up with my own sorry business."

"Of course I'm in deep trouble"—with which Winch came nearer again; "but turning you on was exactly what I wanted."

Mark Monteith, at this, couldn't, for all his rising dismay, but laugh out; his sense of the ridiculous so swallowed up, for that brief convulsion, his sense of the sinister. Of such conivence in pain, it seemed, was the fact of another's pain, and of so much worth again disinterested sympathy! "Your interest was then—?"

"My interest was in your being interesting. For you *are!* And my nerves—!" said Newton Winch with a face from which the mystifying smile had vanished, yet in which distinction, as Mark so persistently appreciated it, still sat in the midst of ravage.

Mark wondered and wondered—he made strange things out. "Your nerves have needed company." He could lay his hand on him now, even as shortly before he had felt Winch's own pressure of possession and detention. "As good for you yourself, that—or still better," he went on—"than I and my grievance were to have found you. Talk to we, talk to we, Newton Winch!" he added with an immense inspiration of charity.

"That's a different matter—that others but too much can do! But I'll say this. If you want to go to Phil Bloodgood—!"

"Well?" said Mark as he stopped. He stopped, and Mark had now a hand on each of his shoulders and held him at arm's-length, held him with a fine idea that was not disconnected from the sight of the small neat weapon he had been fingering in the low luxurious morocco chair—it was of the finest orange colour—and then had laid beside him on the carpet; where, after he had admitted his visitor, his presence of mind coming back to it and suggesting that he couldn't pick it up without making it more conspicuous, he had thought, by some swing of the foot or other casual manoeuvre, to dissimulate its visibility.

They were at close quarters now as not before and Winch perfectly passive, with eyes that somehow had no shadow of a secret left and with the betrayal to the sentient hands that grasped him of an intense, an extraordinary general tremor. To Mark's challenge he opposed afresh a brief silence, but the very quality of it, with his face speaking, was that of a gaping wound. "Well, you needn't take *that* trouble. You see I'm such another."

"Such another as Phil—?"

He didn't blink. "I don't know for sure, but I guess I'm worse."

Henry James

"Do you mean you're guilty—?"

"I mean I shall be wanted. Only I've stayed to take it."

Mark threw back his head, but only tightened his hands. He inexpressibly understood, and nothing in life had ever been so strange and dreadful to him as his thus helping himself by a longer and straighter stretch, as it were, to the monstrous sense of his friend's "education." It had been, in its immeasurable action, the education of business, of which the fruits were all around them. Yet prodigious was the interest, for prodigious truly—it seemed to loom before Mark—must have been the system. "To 'take' it?" he echoed; and then, though faltering a little, "To take what?"

He had scarce spoken when a long sharp sound shrilled in from the outer door, seeming of so high and peremptory a pitch that with the start it gave him his grasp of his host's shoulders relaxed an instant, though to the effect of no movement in *them* but what came from just a sensibly intenser vibration of the whole man. "For *that*!" said Newton Winch.

"Then you've known—?"

"I've expected. You've helped me to wait." And then as Mark gave an ironic wail: "You've tided me over. My condition has *wanted* somebody or something. Therefore, to complete this service, will you be so good as to open the door?"

Deep in the eyes Mark looked him, and still to the detection of no glimmer of the earlier man in the depths. The earlier man had been what he invidiously remembered—yet would *he* had been the whole simpler story! Then he moved his own eyes straight to the chair under which the revolver lay and which was but a couple of yards away. He felt his companion take this consciousness in, and it determined in them another long, mute exchange. "What do you mean to do?"

"Nothing."

"On your honour?"

"*My* 'honour'?" his host returned with an accent that he felt even as it sounded he should never forget.

It brought to his own face a crimson flush—he dropped his guarding hands. Then as for a last look at him: "You're wonderful!"

"We *are* wonderful," said Newton Winch, while, simultaneously with the words, the pressed electric bell again and for a longer time pierced the warm cigaretted air.

Mark turned, threw up his arms, and it was only when he had passed through the vestibule and laid his hand on the door-knob that the horrible noise dropped. The next moment he was face to face with two visitors, a nondescript personage in a high hat and an astrakhan collar and cuffs, and a great belted constable, a splendid massive New York "officer" of the type he had had occasion to wonder at much again in the course of his walk, the type so by itself—his wide observation quite suggested—among those of the peacemakers of the earth. The pair stepped straight in—no word was said; but as he closed the door behind them Mark heard the infallible crack of a discharged pistol and, so nearly with it as to make all one violence, the sound of a great fall; things the effect of which was to lift him, as it were, with his company, across the threshold of the room in a shorter time than that taken by this record of the fact. But their rush availed little; Newton was stretched on his back before the fire; he had held the weapon horribly to his temple, and his upturned face was disfigured. The emissaries of the law, looking down at him, exhaled simultaneously a gruff imprecation, and then while the worthy in the high hat bent over the subject of their visit the one in the helmet raised a severe pair of eyes to Mark. "Don't you think, sir, you might have prevented it?"

Mark took a hundred things in, it seemed to him—things of the scene, of the moment, and of all the strange moments before; but one appearance more vividly even than the others stared out at him. "I really think I must practically have caused it."

CRAPY CORNELIA

I

THREE times within a quarter of an hour—shifting the while
his posture on his chair of contemplation—had he looked at
his watch as for its final sharp hint that he should decide, that
he should get up. His seat was one of a group fairly
sequestered, unoccupied save for his own presence, and from
where he lingered he looked off at a stretch of lawn
freshened by recent April showers and on which sundry
small children were at play. The trees, the shrubs, the plants,
every stem and twig just ruffled as by the first touch of the
light finger of the relenting year, struck him as standing still
in the blest hope of more of the same caress; the quarter
about him held its breath after the fashion of the child who
waits with the rigour of an open mouth and shut eyes for the
promised sensible effect of his having been good. So, in the
windless, sun-warmed air of the beautiful afternoon, the Park
of the winter's end had struck White-Mason as waiting; even
New York, under such an impression, was "good," good
enough—for *him*; its very sounds were faint, were almost
sweet, as they reached him from so seemingly far beyond the
wooded horizon that formed the remoter limit of his large
shallow glade. The tones of the frolic infants ceased to be
nondescript and harsh—were in fact almost as fresh and

Henry James

decent as the frilled and puckered and ribboned garb of the little girls, which had always a way, in those parts, of so portentously flaunting the daughters of the strange native—that is of the overwhelmingly alien—populace at him.

Not that these things in particular were his matter of meditation now; he had wanted, at the end of his walk, to sit apart a little and think—and had been doing that for twenty minutes, even though as yet to no break in the charm of procrastination. But he had looked without seeing and listened without hearing: all that had been positive for him was that he hadn't failed vaguely to feel. He had felt in the first place, and he continued to feel—yes, at forty-eight quite as much as at any point of the supposed reign of younger intensities—the great spirit of the air, the fine sense of the season, the supreme appeal of Nature, he might have said, to his time of life; quite as if she, easy, indulgent, indifferent, cynical Power, were offering him the last chance it would rest with his wit or his blood to embrace. Then with that he had been entertaining, to the point and with the prolonged consequence of accepted immobilization, the certitude that if he did call on Mrs. Worthingham and find her at home he couldn't in justice to himself not put to her the question that had lapsed the other time, the last time, through the irritating and persistent, even if accidental, presence of others. What friends she had—the people who so stupidly, so wantonly stuck! If they *should*, he and she, come to an understanding, that would presumably have to include certain members of her singularly ill-composed circle, in whom it was incredible to him that he should ever take an interest. This defeat, to do himself justice—he had bent rather predominantly on *that*, you see; ideal justice to *her*, with her possible conception of what it should consist of, being another and quite a different matter—he had had the fact of the Sunday afternoon to thank for; she didn't "keep" that day for him, since they hadn't, up to now, quite begun to cultivate the appointment or assignation founded on explicit sacrifices. He might at any rate look to find this pleasant practical Wednesday—should he indeed, at his actual rate, stay it before it ebbed—more liberally and intendingly given him.

The sound he at last most wittingly distinguished in his nook was the single deep note of half-past five borne to him from some high-perched public clock. He finally got up with the sense that the time from then on *ought* at least to be felt as sacred to him. At this juncture it was—while he stood there shaking his garments, settling his hat, his necktie, his shirt-cuffs, fixing the high polish of his fine shoes as if for some reflection in it of his straight and spare and grizzled, his refined and trimmed and dressed, his altogether distinguished person, that of a gentleman abundantly settled, but of a bachelor markedly nervous—at this crisis it was, doubtless, that he at once most measured and least resented his predicament. If he should go he would almost to a certainty find her, and if he should find her he would almost to a certainty come to the point. He wouldn't put it off again—there was that high consideration for him of justice at least to himself. He had never yet denied himself anything so apparently fraught with possibilities as the idea of proposing to Mrs. Worthingham—never yet, in other words, denied himself anything he had so distinctly wanted to do; and the results of that wisdom had remained for him precisely the precious parts of experience. Counting only the offers of his honourable hand, these had been on three remembered occasions at least the consequence of an impulse as sharp and a self-respect as reasoned; a self-respect that hadn't in the least suffered, moreover, from the failure of each appeal. He had been met in the three cases—the only ones he at all compared with his present case—by the frank confession that he didn't somehow, charming as he was, cause himself to be superstitiously believed in; and the lapse of life, afterward, had cleared up many doubts.

It *wouldn't* have done, he eventually, he lucidly saw, each time he had been refused; and the candour of his nature was such that he could live to think of these very passages as a proof of how right he had been—right, that is, to have put himself forward always, by the happiest instinct, only in impossible conditions. He had the happy consciousness of having exposed the important question to the crucial test, and of having escaped, by that persistent logic, a grave mistake. What better proof of his escape than the fact that he was now free to renew the all-interesting inquiry, and should be exactly, about to do so in different and better conditions? The conditions were better by as much more—as much more of his career and character, of his situation, his reputation he could even have called it, of his knowledge of life, of his somewhat extended means, of his possibly augmented charm, of his certainly improved mind and temper—as was involved in the actual impending settlement. Once he had got into motion, once he had crossed the Park and passed out of it, entering, with very little space to traverse, one of the short new streets that abutted on its east side, his step became that of a man young enough to find confidence, quite to find felicity, in the sense, in almost any sense, of action. He could still enjoy almost anything, absolutely an unpleasant thing, in default of a better, that might still remind him he wasn't so old. The standing newness of everything about him would, it was true, have weakened this cheer by too much presuming on it; Mrs. Worthingham's house, before which he stopped, had that gloss of new money, that glare of a piece fresh from the mint and ringing for the first time on any counter, which seems to claim for it, in any transaction, something more than the "face" value.

This could but be yet more the case for the impression of the observer introduced and committed. On our friend's part I mean, after his admission and while still in the hall, the sense of the general shining immediacy, of the still unhushed clamour of the shock, was perhaps stronger than he had ever known it. That broke out from every corner as the high pitch of interest, and with a candour that—no, certainly—he had never seen equalled; every particular expensive object shrieking at him in its artless pride that it had just "come home." He met the whole vision with something of the grimace produced on persons without goggles by the passage from a shelter to a blinding light; and if he had—by a perfectly possible chance—been "snap-shotted" on the spot, would have struck you as showing for his first tribute to the temple of Mrs. Worthingham's charming presence a scowl almost of anguish. He wasn't constitutionally, it may at once be explained for him, a goggled person; and he was condemned, in New York, to this frequent violence of transition—having to reckon with it whenever he went out, as who should say, from himself. The high pitch of interest, to his taste, was the pitch of history, the pitch of acquired and earned suggestion, the pitch of association, in a word; so that he lived by preference, incontestably, if not in a rich gloom, which would have been beyond his means and spirits, at least amid objects and images that confessed to the tone of time.

He had ever felt that an indispensable presence—with a need of it moreover that interfered at no point with his gentle habit, not to say his subtle art, of drawing out what was left him of his youth, of thinly and thriftily spreading the rest of that choicest jam-pot of the cupboard of consciousness over the remainder of a slice of life still possibly thick enough to bear it; or in other words of moving the melancholy limits, the significant signs, constantly a little further on, very much as property-marks or staked boundaries are sometimes stealthily shifted at night. He positively cherished in fact, as against the too inveterate gesture of distressfully guarding his eyeballs—so many New York aspects seemed to keep him at it—an ideal of adjusted appreciation, of courageous curiosity, of fairly letting the world about him, a world of constant breathless renewals and merciless substitutions, make its flaring assault on its own inordinate terms. Newness was value in the piece—for the acquisitor, or at least sometimes might be, even though the act of "blowing" hard, the act marking a heated freshness of arrival, or other form of irruption, could never minister to the peace of those already and long on the field; and this if only because maturer tone was after all most appreciable and most consoling when one staggered back to it, wounded, bleeding, blinded, from the riot of the raw—or, to put the whole experience more prettily, no doubt, from excesses of light.

If he went in, however, with something of his more or less
inevitable scowl, there were really, at the moment, two rather
valid reasons for screened observation; the first of these
being that the whole place seemed to reflect as never before
the lustre of Mrs. Worthingham's own polished and
prosperous little person—to smile, it struck him, with her
smile, to twinkle not only with the gleam of her lovely teeth,
but with that of all her rings and brooches and bangles and
other gewgaws, to curl and spasmodically cluster as in
emulation of her charming complicated yellow tresses, to
surround the most animated of pink-and-white, of ruffled and
ribboned, of frilled and festooned Dresden china shep-
herdesses with exactly the right system of rococo curves and
convolutions and other flourishes, a perfect bower of painted
and gilded and moulded conceits. The second ground of this
immediate impression of scenic extravagance, almost as if
the curtain rose for him to the first act of some small and
expensively mounted comic opera, was that she hadn't, after
all, awaited him in fond singleness, but had again just a trifle
inconsiderately exposed him to the drawback of having to
reckon, for whatever design he might amiably entertain, with
the presence of a third and quite superfluous person, a small
black insignificant but none the less oppressive stranger. It
was odd how, on the instant, the little lady engaged with her
did affect him as comparatively black—very much as if that
had absolutely, in such a medium, to be the graceless
appearance of any item not positively of some fresh shade of
a light colour or of some pretty pretension to a charming
twist. Any witness of their meeting, his hostess should surely
have felt, would have been a false note in the whole rosy
glow; but what note so false as that of the dingy little
presence that she might actually, by a refinement of her
perhaps always too visible study of effect, have provided as a

positive contrast or foil? whose name and intervention, moreover, she appeared to be no more moved to mention and account for than she might have been to "present"—whether as stretched at her feet or erect upon disciplined haunches— some shaggy old domesticated terrier or poodle.

Extraordinarily, after he had been in the room five minutes— a space of time during which his fellow-visitor had neither budged nor uttered a sound—he had made Mrs. Worthingham out as all at once perfectly pleased to see him, completely aware of what he had most in mind, and singularly serene in face of his sense of their impediment. It was as if for all the world she didn't take it for one, the immobility, to say nothing of the seeming equanimity, of their tactless companion; at whom meanwhile indeed our friend himself, after his first ruffled perception, no more adventured a look than if advised by his constitutional kindness that to notice her in any degree would perforce be ungraciously to glower. He talked after a fashion with the woman as to whose power to please and amuse and serve him, as to whose really quite organised and indicated fitness for lighting up his autumn afternoon of life his conviction had lately strained itself so clear; but he was all the while carrying on an intenser exchange with his own spirit and trying to read into the charming creature's behaviour, as he could only call it, some confirmation of his theory that she also had her inward flutter and anxiously counted on him. He found support, happily for the conviction just named, in the idea, at no moment as yet really repugnant to him, the idea bound up in fact with the finer essence of her appeal, that she had her own vision too of her quality and her price, and that the last appearance she would have liked to bristle with was that of being forewarned and eager.

He had, if he came to think of it, scarce definitely warned her, and he probably wouldn't have taken to her so consciously in the first instance without an appreciative sense that, as she was a little person of twenty superficial graces, so she was also a little person with her secret pride. She might just have planted her mangy lion—not to say her muzzled house-dog—there in his path as a symbol that she wasn't cheap and easy; which would be a thing he couldn't possibly wish his future wife to have shown herself in advance, even if to him alone. That she could make him put himself such questions was precisely part of the attaching play of her iridescent surface, the shimmering interfusion of her various aspects; that of her youth with her independence—her pecuniary perhaps in particular, that of her vivacity with her beauty, that of her facility above all with her odd novelty; the high modernity, as people appeared to have come to call it, that made her so much more "knowing" in some directions than even he, man of the world as he certainly was, could pretend to be, though all on a basis of the most unconscious and instinctive and luxurious assumption. She was "up" to everything, aware of everything—if one counted from a short enough time back (from week before last, say, and as if quantities of history had burst upon the world within the fortnight); she was likewise surprised at nothing, and in that direction one might reckon as far ahead as the rest of her lifetime, or at any rate as the rest of his, which was all that would concern him: it was as if the suitability of the future to her personal and rather pampered tastes was what she most took for granted, so that he could see her, for all her Dresden-china shoes and her flutter of wondrous befrilled contemporary skirts, skip by the side of the coming age as over the floor of a ball-room, keeping step with its monstrous stride and prepared for every figure of the dance. Her outlook took form to him suddenly as a great square sunny window that hung in assured fashion over the immensity of life. There rose toward it as from a vast swarming *plaza* a high tide of emotion and sound; yet it was at the same time as if even while he looked her light gemmed hand, flashing on him in addition to those other things the perfect polish of the prettiest pink finger-nails in the world, had touched a spring, the most ingenious of ecent devices for instant ease, which dropped half across the scene a soft-coloured mechanical blind, a fluttered, fringed awning of charmingly toned silk, such as would make a bath of cool shade for the favoured friend leaning with her there—that is for the happy couple itself—on the balcony. The great view would be the prospect and privilege of the very state he coveted—since didn't he covet it?—the state of being so securely at her side; while the wash of privacy, as one might count it, the broad fine brush dipped into clear umber and passed, full and wet, straight across the strong scheme of colour, would represent the security itself, all the uplifted inner elegance, the condition, so ideal, of being shut out from nothing and yet of having, so gaily and breezily aloft, none of the burden or worry of anything. Thus, as I say, for our friend, the place itself, while his vivid impression lasted, portentously opened and spread, and what was before him took, to his vision, though indeed at so other a crisis, the form of the "glimmering square" of the poet; yet, for a still more remarkable fact, with an incongruous object usurping at a given instant the privilege of the frame and seeming, even as he looked, to block the view.

The incongruous object was a woman's head, crowned with a little sparsely feathered black hat, an ornament quite unlike those the women mostly noticed by White-Mason were now "wearing," and that grew and grew, that came nearer and nearer, while it met his eyes, after the manner of images in the kinematograph. It had presently loomed so large that he saw nothing else—not only among the things at a considerable distance, the things Mrs. Worthingham would eventually, yet unmistakably, introduce him to, but among those of this lady's various attributes and appurtenances as to which he had been in the very act of cultivating his consciousness. It was in the course of another minute the most extraordinary thing in the world: everything had altered, dropped, darkened, disappeared; his imagination had spread its wings only to feel them flop all grotesquely at its sides as he recognised in his hostess's quiet companion, the oppressive alien who hadn't indeed interfered with his fanciful flight, though she had prevented his immediate declaration and brought about the thud, not to say the felt violent shock, of his fall to earth, the perfectly plain identity of Cornelia Rasch. It was she who had remained there at attention; it was she their companion hadn't introduced; it was she he had forborne to face with his fear of incivility. He stared at her—everything else went.

"Why it has been *you* all this time?"

Miss Rasch fairly turned pale. "I was waiting to see if you'd know me."

"Ah, my dear Cornelia"—he came straight out with it— "rather!"

"Well, it isn't," she returned with a quick change to red now, "from having taken much time to look at me!"

She smiled, she even laughed, but he could see how she had felt his unconsciousness, poor thing; the acquaintance, quite the friend of his youth, as she had been, the associate of his childhood, of his early manhood, of his middle age in fact, up to a few years back, not more than ten at the most; the associate too of so many of his associates and of almost all of his relations, those of the other time, those who had mainly gone for ever; the person in short whose noted disappearance, though it might have seemed final, had been only of recent seasons. She was present again now, all unexpectedly—he had heard of her having at last, left alone after successive deaths and with scant resources, sought economic salvation in Europe, the promised land of American thrift—she was present as this almost ancient and this oddly unassertive little rotund figure whom one seemed no more obliged to address than if she had been a black satin ottoman "treated" with buttons and gimp; a class of object as to which the policy of blindness was imperative. He felt the need of some explanatory plea, and before he could think had uttered one at Mrs. Worthingham's expense. "Why, you see we weren't introduced—!"

"No—but I didn't suppose I should have to be named to you."

"Well, my dear woman, you haven't—do me that justice!" He could at least make this point. "I felt all the while—!" However, it would have taken him long to say what he had been feeling; and he was aware now of the pretty projected light of Mrs. Worthingham's wonder. She looked as if, out for a walk with her, he had put her to the inconvenience of his stopping to speak to a strange woman in the street.

"I never supposed you knew her!"—it was to him his hostess excused herself.

This made Miss Rasch spring up, distinctly flushed, distinctly strange to behold, but not vulgarly nettled—Cornelia was incapable of that; only rather funnily bridling and laughing, only showing that this was all she had waited for, only saying just the right thing, the thing she could make so clearly a jest. "Of course if you *had* you'd have presented him."

Mrs. Worthingham looked while answering at White-Mason. "I didn't want you to go—which you see you do as soon as he speaks to you. But I never dreamed—!"

"That there was anything between us? Ah, there are no end of things!" He, on his side, though addressing the younger and prettier woman, looked at his fellow-guest; to whom he even continued: "When did you get back? May I come and see you the very first thing?"

Cornelia gasped and wriggled—she practically giggled; she had lost every atom of her little old, her little young, though always unaccountable prettiness, which used to peep so, on the bare chance of a shot, from behind indefensible features, that it almost made watching her a form of sport. He had heard vaguely of her, it came back to him (for there had been no letters; their later acquaintance, thank goodness, hadn't involved that) as experimenting, for economy, and then as settling, to the same rather dismal end, somewhere in England, "at one of those intensely English places, St. Leonards, Cheltenham, Bognor, Dawlish—which, awfully, *was* it?"—and she now affected him for all the world as some small squirming, exclaiming, genteelly conversing old maid of a type vaguely associated with the three-volume novels he used to feed on (besides his so often encountering it in "real life,") during a far-away stay of his own at Brighton. Odder than any element of his ex-gossip's identity itself, however, was the fact that she somehow, with it all, rejoiced his sight. Indeed the supreme oddity was that the manner of her reply to his request for leave to call should have absolutely charmed his attention. She didn't look at him; she only, from under her frumpy, crapy, curiously exotic hat, and with her good little near-sighted insinuating glare, expressed to Mrs. Worthingham, while she answered him, wonderful arch things, the overdone things of a shy woman. "Yes, you may call—but only when this dear lovely lady has done with you!" The moment after which she had gone.

III

Forty minutes later he was taking his way back from the queer miscarriage of his adventure; taking it, with no conscious positive felicity, through the very spaces that had witnessed shortly before the considerable serenity of his assurance. He had said to himself then, or had as good as said it, that, since he might do perfectly as he liked, it couldn't fail for him that he must soon retrace those steps, humming, to all intents, the first bars of a wedding-march; so beautifully had it cleared up that he was "going to like" letting Mrs. Worthingham accept him. He was to have hummed no wedding-march, as it seemed to be turning out—he had none, up to now, to hum; and yet, extraordinarily, it wasn't in the least because she had refused him. Why then hadn't he liked as much as he had intended to like it putting the pleasant act, the act of not refusing him, in her power? Could it all have come from the awkward minute of his failure to decide sharply, on Cornelia's departure, whether or no he would attend her to the door? He hadn't decided at all—what the deuce had been in him?—but had danced to and fro in the room, thinking better of each impulse and then thinking worse. He had hesitated like an ass erect on absurd hind legs between two bundles of hay; the upshot of which must have been his giving the falsest impression. In what way that was to be for an instant considered had their common past committed him to crapy Cornelia? He repudiated with a whack on the gravel any ghost of an obligation.

What he could get rid of with scanter success, unfortunately, was the peculiar sharpness of his sense that, though mystified by his visible flurry—and yet not mystified enough for a sympathetic question either—his hostess had been, on the whole, even more frankly diverted: which was precisely an example of that newest, freshest, finest freedom in her, the air and the candour of assuming, not "heartlessly," not viciously, not even very consciously, but with a bright pampered confidence which would probably end by affecting one's nerves as the most impertinent stroke in the world, that every blest thing coming up for her in any connection was somehow matter for her general recreation. There she was again with the innocent egotism, the gilded and overflowing anarchism, really, of her doubtless quite unwitting but none the less rabid modern note. Her grace of ease was perfect, but it was all grace of ease, not a single shred of it grace of uncertainty or of difficulty—which meant, when you came to see, that, for its happy working, not a grain of provision was left by it to mere manners. This was clearly going to be the music of the future—that if people were but rich enough and furnished enough and fed enough, exercised and sanitated and manicured and generally advised and advertised and made "knowing" enough, *avertis* enough, as the term appeared to be nowadays in Paris, all they had to do for civility was to take the amused ironic view of those who might be less initiated. In *his* time, when he was young or even when he was only but a little less middle-aged, the best manners had been the best kindness, and the best kindness had mostly been some art of not insisting on one's luxurious differences, of concealing rather, for common humanity, if not for common decency, a part at least of the intensity or the ferocity with which one might be "in the know."

Oh, the "know"—Mrs. Worthingham was in it, all instinctively, inevitably, and as a matter of course, up to her eyes; which didn't, however, the least little bit prevent her being as ignorant as a fish of everything that really and intimately and fundamentally concerned *him*, poor dear old White-Mason. She didn't, in the first place, so much as know who he was—by which he meant know who and what it was to *be* a White-Mason, even a poor and a dear and old one, "anyway." That indeed—he did her perfect justice—was of the very essence of the newness and freshness and beautiful, brave, social irresponsibility by which she had originally dazzled him: just exactly that circumstance of her having no instinct for any old quality or quantity or identity, a single historic or social value, as he might say, of the New York of his already almost legendary past; and that additional one of his, on his side, having, so far as this went, cultivated blankness, cultivated positive prudence, as to her own personal background—the vagueness, at the best, with which all honest gentlefolk, the New Yorkers of his approved stock and conservative generation, were content, as for the most part they were indubitably wise, to surround the origins and antecedents and queer unimaginable early influences of persons swimming into their ken from those parts of the country that quite necessarily and naturally figured to their view as "Godforsaken" and generally impossible.

The few scattered surviving representatives of a society once "good"—*rari nantes in gurgite vasto*—were liable, at the pass things had come to, to meet, and even amid old shades once sacred, or what was left of such, every form of social impossibility, and, more irresistibly still, to find these apparitions often carry themselves (often at least in the case of the women) with a wondrous wild gallantry, equally imperturbable and inimitable, the sort of thing that reached its maximum in Mrs. Worthingham. Beyond that who ever wanted to look up their annals, to reconstruct their steps and stages, to dot their i's in fine, or to "go behind" anything that was theirs? One wouldn't do that for the world—a rudimentary discretion forbade it; and yet this check from elementary undiscussable taste quite consorted with a due respect for them, or at any rate with a due respect for oneself in connection with them; as was just exemplified in what would be his own, what would be poor dear old White-Mason's, insurmountable aversion to having, on any pretext, the doubtless very queer spectre of the late Mr.

Worthingham presented to him. No question had he asked, or would he ever ask, should his life—that is should the success of his courtship—even intimately depend on it, either about that obscure agent of his mistress's actual affluence or about the happy head-spring itself, and the apparently copious tributaries, of the golden stream.

From all which marked anomalies, at any rate, what was the moral to draw? He dropped into a Park chair again with that question, he lost himself in the wonder of why he had come away with his homage so very much unpaid. Yet it didn't seem at all, actually, as if he could say or conclude, as if he could do anything but keep on worrying—just in conformity with his being a person who, whether or no familiar with the need to make his conduct square with his conscience and his taste, was never wholly exempt from that of making his taste and his conscience square with his conduct. To this latter occupation he further abandoned himself, and it didn't release him from his second brooding session till the sweet spring sunset had begun to gather and he had more or less cleared up, in the deepening dusk, the effective relation between the various parts of his ridiculously agitating experience. There were vital facts he seemed thus to catch, to seize, with a nervous hand, and the twilight helping, by their vaguely whisked tails; unquiet truths that swarmed out after the fashion of creatures bold only at eventide, creatures that hovered and circled, that verily brushed his nose, in spite of their shyness. Yes, he had practically just sat on with his "mistress"—heaven save the mark!—as if not to come to the point; as if it had absolutely come up that there would be something rather vulgar and awful in doing so. The whole stretch of his stay after Cornelia's withdrawal had been consumed by his almost ostentatiously treating himself to the opportunity of which he was to make nothing. It was as if he had sat and watched himself—that came back to him: Shall I now or sha'n't I? Will I now or won't I? "Say within the next three minutes, say by a quarter past six, or by twenty minutes past, at the furthest—always if nothing more comes up to prevent."

What had already come up to prevent was, in the strangest and drollest, or at least in the most preposterous, way in the world, that not Cornelia's presence, but her very absence, with its distraction of his thoughts, the thoughts that lumbered after her, had made the difference; and without his being the least able to tell why and how. He put it to himself after a fashion by the image that, this distraction once created, his working round to his hostess again, his reverting to the matter of his errand, began suddenly to represent a return from so far. That was simply all—or rather a little less than all; for something else had contributed. "I never dreamed you knew her," and "I never dreamed *you* did," were inevitably what had been exchanged between them— supplemented by Mrs. Worthingham's mere scrap of an explanation: "Oh yes—to the small extent you see. Two years ago in Switzerland when I was at a high place for an 'aftercure,' during twenty days of incessant rain, she was the only person in an hotel full of roaring, gorging, smoking Germans with whom I could have a word of talk. She and I were the only speakers of English, and were thrown together like castaways on a desert island and in a raging storm. She was ill besides, and she had no maid, and mine looked after her, and she was very grateful—writing to me later on and saying she should certainly come to see me if she ever returned to New York. She has returned, you see—and there she was, poor little creature!" Such was Mrs. Worthingham's tribute—to which even his asking her if Miss Rasch had ever happened to speak of him caused her practically to add nothing. Visibly she had never thought again of any one Miss Rasch had spoken of or anything Miss Rasch had said; right as she was, naturally, about her being a little clever queer creature. This was perfectly true, and yet it was probably—by being *all* she could dream of about her—what had paralysed his proper gallantry. Its effect had been not in what it simply stated, but in what, under his secretly disintegrating criticism, it almost luridly symbolised.

He had quitted his seat in the Louis Quinze drawing-room without having, as he would have described it, done anything but give the lady of the scene a superior chance not to betray a defeated hope—not, that is, to fail of the famous "pride" mostly supposed to prop even the most infatuated women at such junctures; by which chance, to do her justice, she had thoroughly seemed to profit. But he finally rose from his later station with a feeling of better success. He had by a happy turn of his hand got hold of the most precious, the least obscure of the flitting, circling things that brushed his ears. What he wanted—as justifying for him a little further consideration—was there before him from the moment he could put it that Mrs. Worthingham had no data. He almost hugged that word,—it suddenly came to mean so much to him. No data, he felt, for a conception of the sort of thing the New York of "his time" had been in his personal life—the New York so unexpectedly, so vividly and, as he might say, so perversely called back to all his senses by its identity with that of poor Cornelia's time: since even she had had a time, small show as it was likely to make now, and his time and hers had been the same. Cornelia figured to him while he walked away as, by contrast and opposition, a massive little bundle of data; his impatience to go to see her sharpened as he thought of this: so certainly should he find out that wherever he might touch her, with a gentle though firm pressure, he would, as the fond visitor of old houses taps and fingers a disfeatured, overpapered wall with the conviction of a wainscot-edge beneath, recognise some small extrusion of history.

IV

There would have been a wonder for us meanwhile in his continued use, as it were, of his happy formula—brought out to Cornelia Rasch within ten minutes, or perhaps only within twenty, of his having settled into the quite comfortable chair that, two days later, she indicated to him by her fireside. He had arrived at her address through the fortunate chance of his having noticed her card, as he went out, deposited, in the good old New York fashion, on one of the rococo tables of Mrs. Worthingham's hall. His eye had been caught by the pencilled indication that was to affect him, the next instant, as fairly placed there for his sake. This had really been his luck, for he shouldn't have liked to write to Mrs. Worthingham for guidance—*that* he felt, though too impatient just now to analyze the reluctance. There was nobody else he could have approached for a clue, and with this reflection he was already aware of how it testified to their rare little position, his and Cornelia's—position as conscious, ironic, pathetic survivors together of a dead and buried society—that there would have been, in all the town, under such stress, not a member of their old circle left to turn to. Mrs. Worthingham had practically, even if accidentally, helped him to knowledge; the last nail in the coffin of the poor dear extinct past had been planted for him by his having thus to reach his antique contemporary through perforation of the newest newness. The note of this particular recognition was in fact the more prescribed to him that the ground of Cornelia's return to a scene swept so bare of the associational charm was certainly inconspicuous. What had she then come back for?—he had asked himself that; with the effect of deciding that it probably would have been, a little, to "look after" her remnant of property. Perhaps she had come to save what little might still remain of that shrivelled interest; perhaps she had been, by those who took

The Finer Grain

care of it for her, further swindled and despoiled, so that she wished to get at the facts. Perhaps on the other hand—it was a more cheerful chance—her investments, decently administered, were making larger returns, so that the rigorous thrift of Bognor could be finally relaxed.

He had little to learn about the attraction of Europe, and rather expected that in the event of his union with Mrs Worthingham he should find himself pleading for it with the competence of one more in the "know" about Paris and Rome, about Venice and Florence, than even she could be. He could have lived on in *his* New York, that is in the sentimental, the spiritual, the more or less romantic visitation of it; but had it been positive for him that he could live on in hers?—unless indeed the possibility of this had been just (like the famous *vertige de l'abime*, like the solicitation of danger, or otherwise of the dreadful) the very hinge of his whole dream. However that might be, his curiosity was occupied rather with the conceivable hinge of poor Cornelia's: it was perhaps thinkable that even Mrs. Worthingham's New York, once it should have become possible again at all, might have put forth to this lone exile a plea that wouldn't be in the chords of Bognor. For himself, after all, too, the attraction had been much more of the Europe over which one might move at one's ease, and which therefore could but cost, and cost much, right and left, than of the Europe adapted to scrimping. He saw himself on the whole scrimping with more zest even in Mrs. Worthingham's New York than under the inspiration of Bognor. Apart from which it was yet again odd, not to say perceptibly pleasing to him, to note where the emphasis of his interest fell in this fumble of fancy over such felt oppositions as the new, the latest, the luridest power of money and the ancient reserves and moderations and mediocrities. These last struck him as showing by contrast the old brown surface and tone as of velvet rubbed and worn, shabby, and even a bit dingy, but all soft and subtle and still velvety—which meant still dignified; whereas the angular facts of current finance were as harsh and metallic and bewildering as some stacked "exhibit" of ugly patented inventions, things his mediaeval mind forbade his taking in. He had for instance the sense of knowing the pleasant little old Rasch fortune—pleasant as far as it went; blurred memories and impressions of what it had been and what it hadn't, of how it had grown and how languished and how melted; they came back to him and put on such vividness that he could almost have figured himself testify for them before a bland and encouraging Board. The idea of taking the field in any manner on the subject of Mrs. Worthingham's resources would have affected him on the other hand as an odious ordeal, some glare of embarrassment and exposure in a circle of hard unhelpful attention, of converging, derisive, unsuggestive eyes.

In Cornelia's small and quite cynically modern flat—the house had a grotesque name, "The Gainsborough," but at least wasn't an awful boarding-house, as he had feared, and she could receive him quite honourably, which was so much to the good—he would have been ready to use at once to her the greatest freedom of friendly allusion: "Have you still your old 'family interest' in those two houses in Seventh Avenue?—one of which was next to a corner grocery, don't you know? and was occupied as to its lower part by a candy-shop where the proportion of the stock of suspectedly stale popcorn to that of rarer and stickier joys betrayed perhaps a modest capital on the part of your father's, your grand-father's, or whoever's tenant, but out of which I nevertheless remember once to have come as out of a bath of sweets, with my very garments, and even the separate hairs of my head, glued together. The other of the pair, a tobacconist's, further down, had before it a wonderful huge Indian who thrust out wooden cigars at an indifferent world—you could buy candy cigars too, at the pop-corn shop, and I greatly preferred them to the wooden; I remember well how I used to gape in fascination at the Indian and wonder if the last of the Mohicans was like him; besides admiring so the resources of a family whose 'property' was in such forms. I haven't been round there lately—we must go round together; but don't tell me the forms have utterly perished!" It was after *that* fashion he might easily have been moved, and with almost no transition, to break out to Cornelia—quite as if taking up some old talk, some old community of gossip, just where they had left it; even with the consciousness perhaps of overdoing a little, of putting at its maximum, for the present harmony, recovery, recapture (what should he call it?) the pitch and quantity of what the past had held for them.

He didn't in fact, no doubt, dart straight off to Seventh Avenue, there being too many other old things and much nearer and long subsequent; the point was only that for everything they spoke of after he had fairly begun to lean back and stretch his legs, and after she had let him, above all, light the first of a succession of cigarettes—for everything they spoke of he positively cultivated extravagance and excess, piling up the crackling twigs as on the very altar of memory; and that by the end of half an hour she had lent herself, all gallantly, to their game. It was the game of feeding the beautiful iridescent flame, ruddy and green and gold, blue and pink and amber and silver, with anything they could pick up, anything that would burn and flicker. Thick-strown with such gleanings the occasion seemed indeed, in spite of the truth that they perhaps wouldn't have proved, under cross-examination, to have rubbed shoulders in the other life so very hard. Casual contacts, qualified communities enough, there had doubtless been, but not particular "passages," nothing that counted, as he might think of it, for their "very own" together, for nobody's else at all. These shades of historic exactitude didn't signify; the more and the less that there had been made perfect terms—and just by his being there and by her rejoicing in it—with their present need to have *had* all their past could be made to appear to have given them. It was to this tune they proceeded, the least little bit as if they knowingly pretended—he giving her the example and setting her the pace of it, and she, poor dear, after a first inevitable shyness, an uncertainty of wonder, a breathlessness of courage, falling into step and going whatever length he would.

She showed herself ready for it, grasping gladly at the perception of what he must mean; and if she didn't immediately and completely fall in—not in the first half-hour, not even in the three or four others that his visit, even whenever he consulted his watch, still made nothing of—she yet understood enough as soon as she understood that, if their finer economy hadn't so beautifully served, he might have been conveying this, that, and the other incoherent and easy thing by the comparatively clumsy method of sound and statement. "No, I never made love to you; it would in fact have been absurd, and I don't care—though I almost know, in the sense of almost remembering!—who did and who didn't; but you were always about, and so was I, and, little as you may yourself care who I did it to, I dare say you remember (in the sense of having known of it!) any old appearances that told. But we can't afford at this time of day not to help each other to have had—well, everything there was, since there's no more of it now, nor any way of coming by it except so; and therefore let us make together, let us make over and recreate, our lost world; for which we have after all and at the worst such a lot of material. You were in particular my poor dear sisters' friend—they thought you the funniest little brown thing possible; so isn't that again to the good? You were mine only to the extent that you were so much in and out of the house—as how much, if we come to that, wasn't one in and out, south of Thirtieth Street and north of Washington Square, in those days, those spacious, sociable, Arcadian days, that we flattered ourselves we filled with the modern fever, but that were so different from any of these arrangements of pretended hourly Time that dash themselves forever to pieces as from the fiftieth floors of sky-scrapers."

This was the kind of thing that was in the air, whether he said it or not, and that could hang there even with such quite other things as more crudely came out; came in spite of its being perhaps calculated to strike us that these last would have been rather and most the unspoken and the indirect. They were Cornelia's contribution, and as soon as she had begun to talk of Mrs. Worthingham—*he* didn't begin it!— they had taken their place bravely in the centre of the circle. There they made, the while, their considerable little figure, but all within the ring formed by fifty other allusions, fitful but really intenser irruptions that hovered and wavered and came and went, joining hands at moments and whirling round as in chorus, only then again to dash at the slightly huddled centre with a free twitch or peck or push or other taken liberty, after the fashion of irregular frolic motions in a country dance or a Christmas game.

"You're so in love with her and want to marry her!"—she said it all sympathetically and yearningly, poor crapy Cornelia; as if it were to be quite taken for granted that she knew all about it. And then when he had asked how she knew—why she took so informed a tone about it; all on the wonder of her seeming so much more "in" it just at that hour than he himself quite felt he could figure for: "Ah, how but from the dear lovely thing herself? Don't you suppose *she* knows it?"

"Oh, she absolutely 'knows' it, does she?"—he fairly heard himself ask that; and with the oddest sense at once of sharply wanting the certitude and yet of seeing the question, of hearing himself say the words, through several thicknesses of some wrong medium. He came back to it from a distance; as he would have had to come back (this was again vivid to him) should he have got round again to his ripe intention three days before—after his now present but then absent friend, that is, had left him planted before his now absent but then present one for the purpose. "Do you mean she—at all confidently!—expects?" he went on, not much minding if it couldn't but sound foolish; the time being given it for him meanwhile by the sigh, the wondering gasp, all charged with the unutterable, that the tone of his appeal set in motion. He saw his companion look at him, but it might have been with the eyes of thirty years ago; when—very likely.—he had put her some such question about some girl long since dead. Dimly at first, then more distinctly, didn't it surge back on him for the very strangeness that there had been some such passage as this between them—yes, about Mary Cardew!—in the autumn of '68?

"Why, don't you realise your situation?" Miss Rasch struck him as quite beautifully wailing—above all to such an effect of deep interest, that is, on her own part and in him.

"My situation?"—he echoed, he considered; but reminded afresh, by the note of the detached, the far-projected in it, of what he had last remembered of his sentient state on his once taking ether at the dentist's.

"Yours and hers—the situation of her adoring you. I suppose you at least know it," Cornelia smiled.

Yes, it was like the other time and yet it wasn't. She was like—poor Cornelia was—everything that used to be; that somehow was most definite to him. Still he could quite reply "Do you call it—her adoring me—*my* situation?"

"Well, it's a part of yours, surely—if you're in love with her."

"Am I, ridiculous old person! in love with her?" White-Mason asked.

"I may be a ridiculous old person," Cornelia returned—"and, for that matter, of course I am! But she's young and lovely and rich and clever: so what could be more natural?"

"Oh, I was applying that opprobrious epithet—!" He didn't finish, though he meant he had applied it to himself. He had got up from his seat; he turned about and, taking in, as his eyes also roamed, several objects in the room, serene and sturdy, not a bit cheap-looking, little old New York objects of '68, he made, with an inner art, as if to recognise them—made so, that is, for himself; had quite the sense for the moment of asking them, of imploring them, to recognise *him*, to be for him things of his own past. Which they truly were, he could have the next instant cried out; for it meant that if three or four of them, small sallow carte-de-visite photographs, faithfully framed but spectrally faded, hadn't in every particular, frames and balloon skirts and false "property" balustrades of unimaginable terraces and all, the tone of time, the secret for warding and easing off the perpetual imminent ache of one's protective scowl, one would verily but have to let the scowl stiffen, or to take up seriously the question of blue goggles, during what might remain of life.

V

What he actually took up from a little old Twelfth-Street table that piously preserved the plain mahogany circle, with never a curl nor a crook nor a hint of a brazen flourish, what he paused there a moment for commerce with, his back presented to crapy Cornelia, who sat taking that view of him, during this opportunity, very protrusively and frankly and fondly, was one of the wasted mementos just mentioned, over which he both uttered and suppressed a small comprehensive cry. He stood there another minute to look at it, and when he turned about still kept it in his hand, only holding it now a litde behind him. "You *must* have come back to stay—with all your beautiful things. What else does it mean?"

"'Beautiful'?" his old friend commented with her brow all wrinkled and her lips thrust out in expressive dispraise. They might at that rate have been scarce more beautiful than she herself. "Oh, don't talk so—after Mrs. Worthingham's! *They're* wonderful, if you will: such things, such things! But one's own poor relics and odds and ends are one's own at least; and one *has*—yes—come back to them. They're all I have in the world to come back to. They were stored, and what I was paying—!" Miss Rasch wofully added.

He had possession of the small old picture; he hovered there; he put his eyes again to it intently; then again held it a little behind him as if it might have been snatched away or the very feel of it, pressed against him, was good to his palm. "Mrs. Worthingham's things? You think them beautiful?"

Cornelia did now, if ever, show an odd face. "Why certainly prodigious, or whatever. Isn't that conceded?"

"No doubt every horror, at the pass we've come to, is conceded. That's just what I complain of."

"Do you *complain?*"—she drew it out as for surprise: she couldn't have imagined such a thing.

"To me her things are awful. They're the newest of the new."

"Ah, but the old forms!"

"Those are the most blatant. I mean the swaggering reproductions."

"Oh but," she pleaded, "we can't all be *really* old."

"No, we can't, Cornelia. But *you* can—!" said White-Mason with the frankest appreciation.

She looked up at him from where she sat as he could imagine her looking up at the curate at Bognor. "Thank you, sir! If that's all you want—!"

"It *is*" he said, "all I want—or almost."

"Then no wonder such a creature as that," she lightly moralised, "won't suit you!"

He bent upon her, for all the weight of his question, his smoothest stare. "You hold she certainly won't suit me?"

"Why, what can I tell about it? Haven't you by this time found out?"

"No, but I think I'm finding." With which he began again to explore.

Miss Rasch immensely wondered. "You mean you don't expect to come to an understanding with her?" And then as even to this straight challenge he made at first no answer: "Do you mean you give it up?"

He waited some instants more, but not meeting her eyes— only looking again about the room. "What do you think of my chance?"

"Oh," his companion cried, "what has what I think to do with it? How can I think anything but that she must like you?"

"Yes—of course. But how much?"

"Then don't you really know?" Cornelia asked.

He kept up his walk, oddly preoccupied and still not looking at her. "Do you, my dear?"

She waited a little. "If you haven't really put it to her I don't suppose she knows."

This at last arrested him again. "My dear Cornelia, she doesn't know—!"

He had paused as for the desperate tone, or at least the large emphasis of it, so that she took him up. "The more reason then to help her to find it out."

"I mean," he explained, "that she doesn't know anything."

"Anything?"

"Anything else, I mean—even if she does know *that*."

Cornelia considered of it. "But what else need she—in

particular—know? Isn't that the principal thing?"

"Well"—and he resumed his circuit—"she doesn't know anything that we know. But nothing," he re-emphasised—"nothing whatever!"

"Well, can't she do without that?"

"Evidently she can—and evidently she does, beautifully. But the question is whether *I* can!"

He had paused once more with his point—but she glared, poor Cornelia, with her wonder. "Surely if you know for yourself—!"

"Ah, it doesn't seem enough for me to know for myself! One wants a woman," he argued—but still, in his prolonged tour, quite without his scowl—"to know *for* one, to know *with* one. That's what you do now," he candidly put to her.

It made her again gape. "Do you mean you want to marry *me?*"

He was so full of what he did mean, however, that he failed even to notice it. "She doesn't in the least know, for instance, how old I am."

"That's because you're so young!"

"Ah, there you are!"—and he turned off afresh and as if almost in disgust. It left her visibly perplexed—though even the perplexed Cornelia was still the exceedingly pointed; but he had come to her aid after another turn. "Remember, please, that I'm pretty well as old as you."

She had all her point at least, while she bridled and blinked, for this. "You're exactly a year and ten months older."

It checked him there for delight. "You remember my birthday?"

She twinkled indeed like some far-off light of home. "I remember every one's. It's a little way I've always had—and that I've never lost."

He looked at her accomplishment, across the room, as at some striking, some charming phenomenon. "Well, *that's* the sort of thing I want!" All the ripe candour of his eyes confirmed it.

What could she do therefore, she seemed to ask him, but repeat her question of a moment before?—which indeed presently she made up her mind to. "Do you want to marry *me?*"

It had this time better success—if the term may be felt in any degree to apply. All his candour, or more of it at least, was in his slow, mild, kind, considering head-shake. "No, Cornelia—not to *marry* you."

His discrimination was a wonder; but since she was clearly treating him now as if everything about him was, so she could as exquisitely meet it. "Not at least," she convulsively smiled, "until you've honourably tried Mrs. Worthingham. Don't you really *mean* to?" she gallantly insisted.

He waited again a little; then he brought out: "I'll tell you presently." He came back, and as by still another mere glance over the room, to what seemed to him so much nearer. "That table was old Twelfth-Street?"

"Everything here was."

"Oh, the pure blessings! With you, ah, with you, I haven't to wear a green shade." And he had retained meanwhile his small photograph, which he again showed himself. "Didn't we talk of Mary Cardew?"

"Why, do you remember it?" She marvelled to extravagance.

"You make me. You connect me with it. You connect it with we." He liked to display to her this excellent use she thus had, the service she rendered. "There are so many connections—there will be so many. I feel how, with you, they must all come up again for me: in fact you're bringing them out already, just while I look at you, as fast as ever you can. The fact that you knew every one—!" he went on; yet as if there were more in that too than he could quite trust himself about.

"Yes, I knew every one," said Cornelia Rasch; but this time with perfect simplicity. "I knew, I imagine, more than you do—or more than you did."

It kept him there, it made him wonder with his eyes on her. "Things about *them*—our people?"

"Our people. Ours only now."

Ah, such an interest as he felt in this—taking from her while, so far from scowling, he almost gaped, all it might mean! "Ours indeed—and it's awfully good they are; or that we're still here for them! Nobody else is—nobody but you: not a cat!"

"Well, I *am* a cat!" Cornelia grinned.

"Do you mean you can tell me things—?" It was too beautiful to believe.

"About what really *was?*" she artfully considered, holding

him immensely now. "Well, unless they've come to you with time; unless you've learned—or found out."

"Oh," he reassuringly cried—reassuringly, it most seemed, for himself—"nothing has come to me with time, everything has gone from me. How can I find out now! What creature has an idea—?"

She threw up her hands with the shrug of old days—the sharp little shrug his sisters used to imitate and that she hadn't had to go to Europe for. The only thing was that he blessed her for bringing it back.

"Ah, the ideas of people now—!"

"Yes, their ideas are certainly not about us" But he ruefully faced it. "We've none the less, however, to live with them."

"With their ideas—?" Cornelia questioned.

"With *them*—these modern wonders; such as they are!" Then he went on: "It must have been to help me you've come back."

She said nothing for an instant about that, only nodding instead at his photograph. "What has become of yours? I mean of *her*."

This time it made him turn pale. "You remember I *have* one?"

She kept her eyes on him. "In a 'pork-pie' hat, with her hair in a long net. That was so 'smart' then; especially with one's skirt looped up, over one's hooped magenta petticoat, in little festoons, and a row of very big onyx beads over one's braided velveteen sack—braided quite plain and very broad, don't you know?"

He smiled for her extraordinary possession of these things—
she was as prompt as if she had had them before her. "Oh,
rather—'don't I know?' You wore brown velveteen, and, on
those remarkably small hands, funny gauntlets—like mine."

"Oh, do *you* remember? But like yours?" she wondered.

"I mean like hers in my photograph." But he came back to
the present picture. "This is better, however, for really
showing her lovely head."

"Mary's head was a perfection!" Cornelia testified.

"Yes—it was better than her heart."

"Ah, don't say that!" she pleaded. "You weren't fair."

"Don't you think I was fair?" It interested him immensely—
and the more that he indeed mightn't have been; which he
seemed somehow almost to hope.

"She didn't think so—to the very end."

"She didn't?"—ah the right things Cornelia said to him! But
before she could answer he was studying again closely the
small faded face. "No, she doesn't, she doesn't. Oh, her
charming sad eyes and the way they say that, across the
years, straight into mine! But I don't know, I don't know!"
White-Mason quite comfortably sighed.

His companion appeared to appreciate this effect. "That's just
the way you used to flirt with her, poor thing. Wouldn't you
like to have it?" she asked.

"This—for my very own?" He looked up delighted. "I really
may?"

"Well, if you'll give me yours. We'll exchange."

"That's a charming idea. We'll exchange. But you must come and get it at my rooms—where you'll see my things."

For a little she made no answer—as if for some feeling. Then she said: "You asked me just now why I've come back."

He stared as for the connection; after which with a smile: "Not to do *that*—?"

She waited briefly again, but with a queer little look. "I can do those things now; and—yes!—that's in a manner why. I came," she then said, "because I knew of a sudden one day—knew as never before—that I was old."

"I see. I see." He quite understood—she had notes that so struck him. "And how did you like it?"

She hesitated—she decided. "Well, if I liked it, it was on the principle perhaps on which some people like high game!"

"High game—that's good!" he laughed. "Ah, my dear, we're 'high'!"

She shook her head. "No, not you—yet. I at any rate didn't want any more adventures," Cornelia said.

He showed their small relic again with assurance. "You wanted *us*. Then here we are. Oh how we can talk!—with all those things you know! You are an invention. And you'll see there are things J know. I shall turn up here—well, daily."

She took it in, but only after a moment answered. "There was something you said just now you'd tell me. Don't you mean to try—?"

"Mrs. Worthingham?" He drew from within his coat his pocket-book and carefully found a place in it for Mary Cardew's carte-de-visite, folding it together with deliberation over which he put it back. Finally he spoke. "No—I've decided. I can't—I don't want to."

Cornelia marvelled—or looked as if she did. "Not for all she has?"

"Yes—I know all she has. But I also know all she hasn't. And, as I told you, she herself doesn't—hasn't a glimmer of a suspicion of it; and never will have."

Cornelia magnanimously thought "No—but she knows other things."

He shook his head as at the portentous heap of them. "Too many—too many. And other indeed—*so* other! Do you know," he went on, "that it's as if *you*—by turning up for me—had brought that home to me?"

"'For you,'" she candidly considered. "But what—since you can't marry me!—can you do with me?"

Well, he seemed to have it all. "Everything. I can live with you—just this way." To illustrate which he dropped into the other chair by her fire; where, leaning back, he gazed at the flame. "I can't give you up. It's very curious. It has come over me as it did over you when you renounced Bognor. That's it—I know it at last, and I see one can like it. I'm 'high.' You needn't deny it. That's my taste. I'm old." And in spite of the considerable glow there of her little household altar he said it without the scowl.

THE BENCH OF DESOLATION

I

SHE had practically, he believed, conveyed the intimation, the horrid, brutal, vulgar menace, in the course of their last dreadful conversation, when, for whatever was left him of pluck or confidence—confidence in what he would fain have called a little more aggressively the strength of his position—he had judged best not to take it up. But this time there was no question of not understanding, or of pretending he didn't; the ugly, the awful words, ruthlessly formed by her lips, were like the fingers of a hand that she might have thrust into her pocket for extraction of the monstrous object that would serve best for—what should he call it?—a gage of battle.

"If I haven't a very different answer from you within the next three days I shall put the matter into the hands of my solicitor, whom it may interest you to know I've already seen. I shall bring an action for 'breach' against you, Herbert Dodd, as sure as my name's Kate Cookham."

There it was, straight and strong—yet he felt he could say for himself, when once it had come, or even, already, just as it was coming, that it turned on, as if she had moved an electric switch, the very brightest light of his own very reasons. There *she* was, in all the grossness of her native indelicacy, in all her essential excess of will and destitution of scruple; and it was the woman capable of that ignoble threat who, his sharper sense of her quality having become so quite deterrent, was now making for him a crime of it that he shouldn't wish to tie himself to her for life. The vivid, lurid thing was the reality, all unmistakable, of her purpose; she had thought her case well out; had measured its odious, specious presentability; had taken, he might be sure, the very best advice obtainable at Properley, where there was always a first-rate promptitude of everything fourth-rate; it was disgustingly certain, in short, that she'd proceed. She was sharp and adroit, moreover—distinctly in certain ways a master-hand; how otherwise, with her so limited mere attractiveness, should she have entangled him? He couldn't shut his eyes to the very probable truth that if she should try it she'd pull it off. She *knew* she would—precisely; and her assurance was thus the very proof of her cruelty. That she had pretended she loved him was comparatively nothing; other women had pretended it, and other women too had really done it; but that she had pretended he could possibly have been right and safe and blest in loving *her*, a creature of the kind who could sniff that squalor of the law-court, of claimed damages and brazen lies and published kisses, of love-letters read amid obscene guffaws, as a positive tonic to resentment, as a high incentive to her course—this was what put him so beautifully in the right It was what might signify in a woman all through, he said to himself, the mere imagination of such machinery. Truly what a devilish conception and what an appalling nature!

But there was no doubt, luckily, either, that he *could* plant his feet the firmer for his now intensified sense of these things. He was to live, it appeared, abominably worried, he was to live consciously rueful, he was to live perhaps even what a scoffing world would call abjectly exposed; but at least he was to live saved. In spite of his clutch of which steadying truth, however, and in spite of his declaring to her, with many other angry protests and pleas, that the line of conduct she announced was worthy of a vindictive barmaid, a lurking fear in him, too deep to counsel mere defiance, made him appear to keep open a little, till he could somehow turn round again, the door of possible composition. He had scoffed at her claim, at her threat, at her thinking she could hustle and bully him—"Such a way, my eye, to call back to life a dead love!"—yet his instinct was ever, prudentially but helplessly, for gaining time, even if time only more wofully to quake, and he gained it now by not absolutely giving for his ultimatum that he wouldn't think of coming round. He didn't in the smallest degree mean to come round, but it was characteristic of him that he could for three or four days breathe a little easier by having left her under the impression that he perhaps might. At the same time he couldn't not have said—what had conduced to bring out, in retort, her own last word, the word on which they had parted—"Do you mean to say you yourself would now be *willing* to marry and live with a man of whom you could feel, the thing done, that he'd be all the while thinking of you in the light of a hideous coercion?" "Never you mind about *my* willingness," Kate had answered; "you've known what that has been for the last six months. Leave that to me, my willingness—I'll take care of it all right; and just see what conclusion you can come to about your own."

He was to remember afterward how he had wondered whether, turned upon her in silence while her odious lucidity reigned unchecked, his face had shown her anything like the quantity of hate he felt. Probably not at all; no man's face *could* express that immense amount; especially the fair, refined, intellectual, gentlemanlike face which had had—and by her own more than once repeated avowal—so much to do with the enormous fancy she had originally taken to him. "Which—frankly now—would you personally *rather* I should do," he had at any rate asked her with an intention of supreme irony: "just sordidly marry you on top of this, or leave you the pleasure of your lovely appearance in court and of your so assured (since that's how you feel it) big haul of damages? Sha'n't you be awfully disappointed, in fact, if I don't let you get something better out of me than a poor plain ten-shilling gold ring and the rest of the blasphemous rubbish, as we should make it between us, pronounced at the altar? I take it of course," he had swaggered on, "that your pretension wouldn't be for a moment that I should—after the act of profanity—take up my life with you."

"It's just as much my dream as it ever was, Herbert Dodd, to take up mine with *you!* Remember for me that I can do with it, my dear, that my idea is for even as much as that of you!" she had cried; "remember that for me, Herbert Dodd; remember, remember!"

It was on this she had left him—left him frankly under a mortal chill. There might have been the last ring of an appeal or a show of persistent and perverse tenderness in it, however preposterous any such matter; but in point of fact her large, clean, plain, brown face—so much too big for her head, he now more than ever felt it to be, just as her head was so much too big for her body, and just as her hats had an irritating way of appearing to decline choice and conformity in respect to *any* of her dimensions—presented itself with about as much expression as his own shop-window when the broad, blank, sallow blind was down. He was fond of his shop-window with some good show on; he had a fancy for a good show and was master of twenty different schemes of taking arrangement for the old books and prints, "high-class rarities" his modest catalogue called them, in which he dealt and which his maternal uncle, David Geddes, had, as he liked to say, "handed down" to him. His widowed mother had screwed the whole thing, the stock and the connection and the rather bad little house in the rather bad little street, out of the ancient worthy, shortly before his death, in the name of the youngest and most interesting, the "delicate" one and the literary, of her five scattered and struggling children. He could enjoy his happiest collocations and contrasts and effects, his harmonies and varieties of toned and faded leather and cloth, his sought color-notes and the high clearnesses, here and there, of his white and beautifully figured price-labels, which pleased him enough in themselves almost to console him for not oftener having to break, on a customer's insistence, into the balanced composition. But the dropped expanse of time-soiled canvas, the thing of Sundays and holidays, with just his name, "Herbert Dodd, Successor," painted on below his uncle's antique style, the feeble penlike flourishes already quite archaic—this ugly vacant mask, which might so easily be taken for the mask of failure, somehow always gave him a chill.

That had been just the sort of chill—the analogy was complete—of Kate Cookham's last look. He supposed people doing an awfully good and sure and steady business, in whatever line, could see a whole front turned to vacancy that way and merely think of the hours off represented by it. Only for this—nervously to bear it, in other words, and Herbert Dodd, quite with the literary temperament himself, was capable of that amount of play of fancy, or even of morbid analysis—you had to be on some footing, you had to feel some confidence, pretty different from his own up to now. He had never *not* enjoyed passing his show on the other side of the street and taking it in thence with a casual obliquity; but he had never held optical commerce with the drawn blind for a moment longer than he could help. It *always* looked horribly final and as if it never would come up again. Big and bare, with his name staring at him from the middle, it thus offered in its grimness a turn of comparison for Miss Cookham's ominous visage. She never wore pretty, dotty, transparent veils, as Nan Drury did, and the words "Herbert Dodd"—save that she had sounded them at him there two or three times more like a Meg Merrilies or the bold bad woman in one of the melodramas of high life given during the fine season in the pavilion at the end of Properley Pier— were dreadfully, were permanently, seated on her lips. *She* was grim, no mistake.

That evening, alone in the back room above the shop, he saw so little what he could do that, consciously demoralised for the hour, he gave way to tears about it. Her taking a stand so incredibly "low," that was what he couldn't get over. The particular bitterness of his cup was his having let himself in for a struggle on such terms—the use, on her side, of the vulgarest process known to the law: the vulgarest, the vulgarest, he kept repeating that, clinging to the help rendered him by this imputation to his terrorist of the vice he sincerely believed he had ever, among difficulties (for oh he recognised the difficulties!) sought to keep most alien to him. He knew what he was, in a dismal, down-trodden sphere enough—the lean young proprietor of an old business that had itself rather shrivelled with age than ever grown fat, the purchase and sale of second-hand books and prints, with the back street of a long-fronted south-coast watering-place (Old Town by good luck) for the dusky field of his life. But he had gone in for all the education he could get—his educated customers would often hang about for more talk by the half-hour at a time, he actually feeling himself, and almost with a scruple, hold them there; which meant that he had had (he couldn't be blind to that) natural taste and had lovingly cultivated and formed it. Thus, from as far back as he could remember, there had been things all round him that he suffered from when other people didn't; and he had kept most of his suffering to himself—which had taught him, in a manner, *how* to suffer, and how almost to like to.

So, at any rate, he had never let go his sense of certain differences, he had done everything he could to keep it up—whereby everything that was vulgar was on the wrong side of his line. He had believed, for a series of strange, oppressed months, that Kate Cookham's manners and tone were on the right side; she had been governess—for young children—in two very good private families, and now had classes in literature and history for bigger girls who were sometimes brought by their mammas; in fact, coming in one day to look over his collection of students' manuals, and drawing it out, as so many did, for the evident sake of his conversation, she had appealed to him that very first time by her apparently pronounced intellectual side—goodness knew she didn't even then by the physical!—which she had artfully kept in view till she had entangled him past undoing. And it had all been but the cheapest of traps—when he came to take the pieces apart a bit—laid over a brazen avidity. What he now collapsed for, none the less—what he sank down on a chair at a table and nursed his weak, scared sobs in his resting arms for—was the fact that, whatever the trap, it held him as with the grip of sharp murderous steel. There he was, there he was; alone in the brown summer dusk—brown through *his* windows—he cried and he cried. He shouldn't get out without losing a limb. The only question was which of his limbs it should be.

Before he went out, later on—for he at last felt the need to—he could, however, but seek to remove from his face and his betraying eyes, over his washing-stand, the traces of his want of fortitude. He brushed himself up; with which, catching his stricken image a bit spectrally in an old dim toilet-glass, he knew again, in a flash, the glow of righteous resentment. Who should be assured against coarse usage if a man of his really elegant, perhaps in fact a trifle over-refined or "effete" appearance, his absolutely gentlemanlike type, couldn't be? He never went so far as to rate himself, with exaggeration, a gentleman; but he would have maintained against all comers, with perfect candour and as claiming a high advantage, that he was, in spite of that liability to blubber, "like" one; which he *was* no doubt, for that matter, at several points. Like what lady then, who could ever possibly have been taken for one, was Kate Cookham, and therefore how could one have anything—anything of the intimate and private order—out with her fairly and on the plane, the only possible one, of common equality? He might find himself crippled for life; he believed verily, the more he thought, that that was what was before him. But be ended by seeing this doom in the almost redeeming light of the fact that it would all have been because he was, comparatively, too aristocratic. Yes, a man in his station couldn't afford to carry that so far—it must sooner or later, in one way or another, spell ruin. Never mind—it was the only thing he could be. Of course he should exquisitely suffer—but when hadn't he exquisitely suffered? How was he going to get through life by *any* arrangement without that? No wonder such a woman as Kate Cookham had been keen to annex so rare a value. The right thing would have been that the highest price should be paid for it—by such a different sort of logic from this nightmare of *his* having to pay.

II

Which was the way, of course, he talked to Nan Drury—as
he had felt the immediate wild need to do; for he should
perhaps be able to bear it all somehow or other with *her*—
while they sat together, when time and freedom served, on
one of the very last, the far westward, benches of the
interminable sea-front. It wasn't every one who walked so
far, especially at that flat season—the only ghost of a bustle
now, save for the gregarious, the obstreperous haunters of
the fluttering, far-shining Pier, being reserved for the sunny
Parade of midwinter. It wasn't every one who cared for the
sunsets (which you got awfully well from there and which
were a particular strong point of the lower, the more
"sympathetic," as Herbert Dodd liked to call it, Properley
horizon) as he had always intensely cared, and as he had
found Nan Drury care; to say nothing of his having also
observed how little they directly spoke to Miss Cookham. He
had taught this oppressive companion to notice them a bit, as
he had taught her plenty of other things, but that was a
different matter; for the reason that the "land's end"
(stretching a point it carried off that name) had been, and had
had to be, by their lack of more sequestered resorts and
conveniences, the scene of so much of what she styled their
wooing-time—or, to put it more properly, of the time during
which she had made the straightest and most unabashed love
to *him*: just as it could henceforth but render possible, under
an equal rigour, that he should enjoy there periods of
consolation from beautiful, gentle, tender-souled Nan, to
whom he was now at last, after the wonderful way they had
helped each other to behave, going to make love, absolutely
unreserved and abandoned, absolutely reckless and romantic
love, a refuge from poisonous reality, as hard as ever he
might.

The league-long, paved, lighted, garden-plotted, seated and
refuged Marina renounced its more or less celebrated
attractions to break off short here; and an inward curve of the
kindly westward shore almost made a wide-armed bay, with
all the ugliness between town and country, and the further
casual fringe of the coast, turning, as the day waned, to rich
afternoon blooms of grey and brown and distant—it might
fairly have been beautiful Hampshire—blue. Here it was
that, all that blighted summer, with Nan—from the dreadful
May-day on—he gave himself up to the reaction of intimacy
with the *kind* of woman, at least, that he liked; even if of
everything else that might make life possible he was to be,
by what he could make out, forever starved. Here it was
that—as well as on whatever other scraps of occasions they
could manage—Nan began to take off and fold up and put
away in her pocket her pretty, dotty, becoming veil; as under
the logic of his having so tremendously ceased, in the shake
of his dark storm-gust, to be engaged to another woman. Her
removal of that obstacle to a trusted friend's assuring himself
whether the peachlike bloom' of her finer facial curves bore
the test of such further inquiry into their cool sweetness as
might reinforce a mere baffled gaze—her momentous,
complete surrender of so much of her charm, let us say, both
marked the change in the situation of the pair and established
the record of their perfect observance of every propriety for
so long before. They afterward in fact could have dated it,
their full clutch of their freedom and the bliss of their having
so little henceforth to consider save their impotence, their
poverty, their ruin; dated it from the hour of his recital to her
of the—at the first blush—quite appalling upshot of his
second and conclusive "scene of violence" with the mistress
of his fortune, when the dire terms of his release had had to
be formally, and oh! so abjectly, acceded to. She
"compromised," the cruel brute, for Four Hundred Pounds
down—for not a farthing less would she stay her strength
from "proceedings." No jury in the land but would give her

six, on the nail ("Oh she knew quite where she was, thank you!") and he might feel lucky to get off with so whole a skin. This was the sum, then, for which he had grovellingly compounded—under an agreement sealed by a supreme exchange of remarks.

"'Where in the name of lifelong ruin are you to *find* Four Hundred?'" Miss Cookham had mockingly repeated after him while he gasped as from the twist of her grip on his collar. "That's *your* look-out, and I should have thought you'd have made sure you knew before you decided on your base perfidy." And then she had mouthed and minced, with ever so false a gentility, her consistent, her sickening conclusion. "Of course—I may mention again—if you too distinctly object to the trouble of looking, you know where to find *me*."

"I had rather starve to death than ever go within a mile of you!" Herbert described himself as having sweetly answered; and that was accordingly where *they* devotedly but desperately were—he and she, penniless Nan Drury. Her father, of Drury & Dean, was, like so far too many other of the anxious characters who peered through the dull window-glass of dusty offices at Properley, an Estate and House Agent, Surveyor, Valuer and Auctioneer; she was the prettiest of six, with two brothers, neither of the least use, but, thanks to the manner in which their main natural protector appeared to languish under the accumulation of his attributes, they couldn't be said very particularly or positively to live. Their continued collective existence was a good deal of a miracle even to themselves, though they had fallen into the way of not unnecessarily, or too nervously, exchanging remarks upon it, and had even in a sort, from year to year, got used to it. Nan's brooding pinkness when he talked to her, her so very parted lips, considering her pretty teeth, her so very parted eyelids, considering her pretty eyes, all of which might have been those of some waxen image of uncritical faith, cooled the heat of his helplessness very much as if he were laying his head on a tense silk pillow. She had, it was true, forms of speech, familiar watchwords, that affected him as small scratchy perforations of the smooth surface from within; but his pleasure in her and need of her were independent of such things and really almost altogether determined by the fact of the happy, even if all so lonely, forms and instincts in her which claimed kinship with his own. With her natural elegance stamped on her as by a die, with her dim and disinherited individual refinement of grace, which would have made any one wonder who she was anywhere—hat and veil and feather-boa and smart umbrella-knob and all—with her regular God-given distinction of type, in fine, she couldn't abide vulgarity much more than he could.

Therefore it didn't seem to him, under his stress, to matter particularly, for instance, if she *would* keep on referring so many things to the time, as she called it, when she came into his life—his own great insistence and contention being that she hadn't in the least entered there till his mind was wholly made up to eliminate his other friend. What that methodical fury was so fierce to bring home to him was the falsity to herself involved in the later acquaintance; whereas just his precious right to hold up his head to everything—before himself at least—sprang from the fact that she couldn't make dates fit anyhow. He hadn't so much as heard of his true beauty's existence (she had come back but a few weeks before from her two years with her terribly trying deceased aunt at Swindon, previous to which absence she had been an unnoticeable chit) till days and days, ever so many, upon his honour, after he had struck for freedom by his great first backing-out letter—the precious document, the treat for a British jury, in which, by itself, Miss Cookham's firm instructed her to recognise the prospect of a fortune. The way the ruffians had been "her" ruffians—it appeared as if she had posted them behind her from the first of her beginning her game!—and the way "instructions" bounced out, with it, at a touch, larger than life, as if she had arrived with her pocket full of them! The date of the letter, taken with its other connections, and the date of *her* first give-away for himself, his seeing her get out of the Brighton train with Bill Frankle that day he had gone to make the row at the Station parcels' office about the miscarriage of the box from Wales—those were the facts it sufficed him to point to, as he had pointed to them for Nan Drury's benefit, goodness knew, often and often enough. If he didn't seek occasion to do so for any one else's—in open court as they said—that was his own affair, or at least his and Nan's.

It little mattered, meanwhile, if on their bench of desolation, all that summer—and it may be added for summers and summers, to say nothing of winters, there and elsewhere, to come—she did give way to her artless habit of not contradicting him enough, which led to her often trailing up and down before him, too complacently, the untimely shreds and patches of his own glooms and desperations. "Well, I'm glad I *am* in your life, terrible as it is, however or whenever I did come in!" and "*Of course* you'd rather have starved—and it seems pretty well as if we shall, doesn't it?—than have bought her off by a false, abhorrent love, wouldn't you?" and "It isn't as if she hadn't made up to you the way she did before you had so much as looked at her, is it? or as if you hadn't shown her what you felt her really to be before you had so much as looked at *me*, is it either?" and "Yes, how on earth, pawning the shoes on your feet, you're going to raise another shilling—*that's* what you want to know, poor darling, don't you?"

III

His creditor, at the hour it suited her, transferred her base of operations to town, to which impenetrable scene she had also herself retired; and his raising of the first Two Hundred, during five exasperated and miserable months, and then of another Seventy piecemeal, bleedingly, after long delays and under the epistolary whiplash cracked by the London solicitor in his wretched ear even to an effect of the very report of Miss Cookham's tongue—these melancholy efforts formed a scramble up an arduous steep where steps were planted and missed, and bared knees were excoriated, and clutches at wayside tufts succeeded and failed, on a system to which poor Nan could have intelligently entered only if she had been somehow less ladylike. She kept putting into his mouth the sick quaver of where he should find the rest, the always inextinguishable rest, long after he had in silent rage fallen away from any further payment at all—at first, he had but too blackly felt, for himself, to the still quite possible non-exclusion of some penetrating ray of "exposure." He didn't care a tuppenny damn now, and in point of fact, after he had by hook and by crook succeeded in being able to unload to the tune of Two-Hundred-and-Seventy, and then simply returned the newest reminder of his outstanding obligation unopened, this latter belated but real sign of fight, the first he had risked, remarkably caused nothing at all to happen; nothing at least but his being moved to quite tragically rueful wonder as to whether exactly some such demonstration mightn't have served his turn at an earlier stage.

He could by this time at any rate measure his ruin—with three fantastic mortgages on his house, his shop, his stock, and a burden of interest to carry under which his business simply stretched itself inanimate, without strength for a protesting kick, without breath for an appealing groan. Customers lingering for further enjoyment of the tasteful remarks he had cultivated the unobstrusive art of throwing in, would at this crisis have found plenty to repay them, might his wit have strayed a little more widely still, toward a circuitous egotistical outbreak, from the immediate question of the merits of this and that author or of the condition of this and that volume. He had come to be conscious through it all of strangely glaring at people when they tried to haggle—and not, as formerly, with the glare of derisive comment on their overdone humour, but with that of fairly idiotised surrender—as if they were much mistaken in supposing, for the sake of conversation, that he might take himself for saveable by the difference between sevenpence and ninepence. He watched everything impossible and deplorable happen as in an endless prolongation of his nightmare; watched himself proceed, that is, with the finest, richest incoherence, to the due preparation of his catastrophe. Everything came to seem *equally* part of this—in complete defiance of proportion; even his final command of detachment, on the bench of desolation (where each successive fact of his dire case regularly cut itself out black, yet of senseless silhouette, against the red west) in respect to poor Nan's flat infelicities, which for the most part kept no pace with the years or with change, but only shook like hard peas in a child's rattle, the same peas a ways, of course, so long as the rattle didn't split open with usage or from somebody's act of irritation. They represented, or they had long done so, her contribution to the more superficial of the two branches of intimacy—the intellectual alternative, the one that didn't merely consist of her preparing herself for his putting his arm round her waist.

There were to have been moments, nevertheless, all the first couple of years, when she did touch in him, though to his actively dissimulating it, a more or less sensitive nerve—moments as they were too, to do her justice, when she treated him not to his own wisdom, or even folly, served up cold, but to a certain small bitter fruit of her personal, her unnatural, plucking. "I wonder that since *she* took legal advice so freely, to come down on you, you didn't take it yourself, a little, before being so sure you stood no chance. Perhaps *your* people would have been sure of something quite different—*perhaps*, I only say, you know." She "only" said it, but she said it, none the less, in the early time, about once a fortnight. In the later, and especially after their marriage, it had a way of coming up again to the exclusion, as it seemed to him, of almost everything else; in fact during the most dismal years, the three of the loss of their two children, the long stretch of sordid embarrassment ending in her death, he was afterward to think of her as having generally said it several times a day. He was then also to remember that his answer, before she had learnt to discount it, had been inveterately at hand: "What would any solicitor have done or wanted to do but drag me just into the hideous public arena"—he had always so put it—"that it has been at any rate my pride and my honour, the one rag of self-respect covering my nakedness, to have loathed and avoided from every point of view?"

That had disposed of it so long as he cared, and by the time he had ceased to care for anything it had also lost itself in the rest of the vain babble of home. After his wife's death, during his year of mortal solitude, it awoke again as an echo of far-off things—far-off, very far-off, because he felt then not ten but twenty years older. That was by reason simply of the dead weight with which his load of debt had settled—the persistence of his misery dragging itself out. With all that had come and gone the bench of desolation was still there, just as the immortal flush of the westward sky kept hanging its indestructible curtain. He had never got away—everything had left him, but he himself had been able to turn his back on nothing—and now, his day's labour before a dirty desk at the Gas Works ended, he more often than not, almost any season at temperate Properley serving his turn, took his slow straight way to the Land's End and, collapsing there to rest, sat often for an hour at a time staring before him. He might in these sessions, with his eyes on the grey-green sea, have been counting again and still recounting the beads, almost all worn smooth, of his rosary of pain—which had for the fingers of memory and the recurrences of wonder the same felt break of the smaller ones by the larger that would have aided a pious mumble in some dusky altar-chapel.

If it has been said of him that when once full submersion, as from far back, had visibly begun to await him, he watched himself, in a cold lucidity, *do* punctually and necessarily each of the deplorable things that were inconsistent with his keeping afloat, so at present again he might have been held agaze just by the presented grotesqueness of that vigil. Such ghosts of dead seasons were all he *had* now to watch—such a recaptured sense for instance as that of the dismal unavailing awareness that had attended his act of marriage. He had let submersion final and absolute become the signal for it—a mere minor determinant having been the more or less contemporaneously unfavourable effect on the business of Drury & Dean of the sudden disappearance of Mr. Dean with the single small tin box into which the certificates of the firm's credit had been found to be compressible. That had been his only form—or had at any rate seemed his only one. He couldn't not have married, no doubt, just as he couldn't not have suffered the last degree of humiliation and almost of want, or just as his wife and children couldn't not have died of the little he was able, under dire reiterated pinches, to do for them; but it was "rum," for final solitary brooding, that he hadn't appeared to see his way definitely to undertake the support of a family till the last scrap of his little low-browed, high-toned business, and the last figment of "property" in the old tiled and timbered shell that housed it, had been sacrificed to creditors mustering six rows deep.

Of course what had counted too in the odd order was that even at the end of the two or three years he had "allowed" her, Kate Cookham, gorged with his unholy tribute, had become the subject of no successful siege on the part either of Bill Frankle or, by what he could make out, of any one else. She had judged decent—he could do her that justice—to take herself personally out of his world, as he called it, for good and all, as soon as he had begun regularly to bleed; and, to whatever lucrative practice she might be devoting her great talents in London or elsewhere, he felt his conscious curiosity about her as cold, with time, as the passion of vain protest that she had originally left him to. He could recall but two direct echoes of her in all the bitter years—both communicated by Bill Frankle, disappointed and exposed and at last quite remarkably ingenuous sneak, who had also, from far back, taken to roaming the world, but who, during a period, used fitfully and ruefully to reappear. Herbert Dodd had quickly seen, at their first meeting—every one met every one sooner or later at Properley, if meeting it could always be called, either in the glare or the gloom of the explodedly attractive Embankment—that no silver stream of which he himself had been the remoter source could have played over the career of this all but repudiated acquaintance. That hadn't fitted with his first, his quite primitive raw vision of the probabilities, and he had further been puzzled when, much later on, it had come to him in a roundabout way that Miss Cookham was supposed to be, or to have been, among them for a few days "on the quiet," and that Frankle, who had seen her and who claimed to know more about it than he said, was cited as authority for the fact. But he hadn't himself at this juncture seen Frankle; he had only wondered, and a degree of mystification had even remained.

That memory referred itself to the dark days of old Drury's smash, the few weeks between his partner's dastardly flight and Herbert's own comment on it in the form of his standing up with Nan for the nuptial benediction of the Vicar of St. Bernard's on a very cold, bleak December morning and amid a circle of seven or eight long-faced, red-nosed and altogether dowdy persons. Poor Nan herself had come to affect him as scarce other than red-nosed and dowdy by that time, but this only added, in his then, and indeed in his lasting view, to his general and his particular morbid bravery. He had cultivated ignorance, there were small inward immaterial luxuries he could scrap-pily cherish even among other, and the harshest, destitutions; and one of them was represented by this easy refusal of his mind to render to certain passages of his experience, to various ugly images, names, associations, the homage of continued attention. That served him, that helped him; but what happened when, a dozen dismal years having worn themselves away, he sat single and scraped bare again, as if his long wave of misfortune had washed him far beyond everything and then conspicuously retreated, was that, thus stranded by tidal action, deposited in the lonely hollow of his fate, he felt even sustaining pride turn to nought and heard no challenge from it when old mystifications, stealing forth in the dusk of the day's work done, scratched at the door of speculation and hung about, through the idle hours, for irritated notice.

The evenings of his squalid clerkship were all leisure now, but there was nothing at all near home on the other hand, for his imagination, numb and stiff from its long chill, to begin to play with. Voices from far off would quaver to him therefore in the stillness; where he knew for the most recurrent, little by little, the faint wail of his wife. He had become deaf to it in life, but at present, after so great an interval, he listened again, listened and listened, and seemed to hear it sound as by the pressure of some weak broken spring. It phrased for his ear her perpetual question, the one she had come to at the last as under the obsession of a discovered and resented wrong, a wrong withal that had its source much more in his own action than anywhere else. "That you didn't make *sure* she could have done anything, that you didn't make sure and that you were too afraid!"—this commemoration had ended by playing such a part of Nan's finally quite contracted consciousness as to exclude everything else.

At the time, somehow, he had made his terms with it; he had then more urgent questions to meet than that of the poor creature's taste in worrying pain; but actually it struck him—not the question, but the fact itself of the taste—as the one thing left over from all that had come and gone. So it was; nothing remained to him in the world, on the bench of desolation, but the option of taking up that echo—together with an abundance of free time for doing so. That he hadn't made sure of what might and what mightn't have been done to him, that he had been too afraid—had the proposition a possible bearing on his present apprehension of things? To reply indeed he would have had to be able to say what his present apprehension of things, left to itself, amounted to; an uninspiring effort indeed he judged it, sunk to so poor a pitch was his material of thought—though it might at last have been the feat he sought to perform as he stared at the grey-green sea.

IV

It was seldom he was disturbed in any form of sequestered speculation, or that at his times of predilection, especially that of the long autumn blankness between the season of trippers and the season of Bath-chairs, there were westward stragglers enough to jar upon his settled sense of priority. For himself his seat, the term of his walk, was consecrated; it had figured to him for years as the last (though there were others, not immediately near it, and differently disposed, that might have aspired to the title); so that he could invidiously distinguish as he approached, make out from a distance any accident of occupation, and never draw nearer while that unpleasantness lasted. What he disliked was to compromise on his tradition, whether for a man, a woman or a connoodling couple; it was to idiots of this last composition he most objected, he having sat there, in the past, alone, having sat there interminably with Nan, having sat there with—well, with other women when women, at hours of ease, could still care or count for him, but having never shared the place with any shuffling or snuffling stranger. It was a world of fidgets and starts, however, the world of his present dreariness—he alone possessed in it, he seemed to make out, of the secret, of the dignity of sitting still with one's fate; so that if he took a turn about or rested briefly elsewhere even foolish philanderers—though this would never have been his and Nan's way—ended soon by some adjournment as visibly pointless as their sprawl. Then, their backs turned, he would drop down on it, the bench of desolation—which was what he, and he only, made it by sad adoption; where, for that matter, moreover, once he had settled at his end, it was marked that nobody else ever came to sit. He saw people, along the Marina, take this liberty with other resting presences; but his own struck them perhaps in general as either of too grim or just of too dingy a vicinage.

He might have affected the fellow-lounger as a man evil, unsociable, possibly engaged in working out the idea of a crime; or otherwise, more probably—for on the whole he surely looked harmless—devoted to the worship of some absolutely unpractical remorse.

On a certain October Saturday he had got off, as usual, early; but the afternoon light, his pilgrimage drawing to its aim, could still show him, at long range, the rare case of an established usurper. His impulse was then, as by custom, to deviate a little and wait, all the more that the occupant of the bench was a lady, and that ladies, when alone, were—at that austere end of the varied frontal stretch—markedly discontinuous; but he kept on at sight of this person's rising, while he was still fifty yards off, and proceeding, her back turned, to the edge of the broad terrace, the outer line of which followed the interspaced succession of seats and was guarded by an iron rail from the abruptly lower level of the beach. Here she stood before the sea, while our friend on his side, recognising no reason to the contrary, sank into the place she had quitted. There were other benches, eastward and off by the course of the drive, for vague ladies. The lady indeed thus thrust upon Herbert's vision might have struck an observer either as not quite vague or as vague with a perverse intensity suggesting design.

Not that our own observer at once thought of these things; he only took in, and with no great interest, that the obtruded presence was a "real" lady; that she was dressed—he noticed such matters—with a certain elegance of propriety or intention of harmony; and that she remained perfectly still for a good many minutes; so many in fact that he presently ceased to heed her, and that as she wasn't straight before him, but as far to the left as was consistent with his missing her profile, he had turned himself to one of his sunsets again (though it wasn't quite one of his best) and let it hold him for a time that enabled her to alter her attitude and present a fuller view. Without other movement, but her back now to the sea and her face to the odd person who had appropriated her corner, she had taken a sustained look at him before he was aware she had stirred. On that apprehension, however, he became also promptly aware of her direct, her applied observation. As his sense of this quickly increased he wondered who she was and what she wanted—what, as it were, was the matter with her; it suggested to him, the next thing, that she had, under some strange idea, actually been waiting for him. Any idea about him to-day on the part of any one could only be strange.

Yes, she stood there with the ample width of the Marina between them, but turned to him, for all the world, as to show frankly that she was concerned with him. And she *was*—oh yes—a real lady: a middle-aged person, of good appearance and of the best condition, in quiet but "handsome" black, save for very fresh white kid gloves, and with a pretty, dotty, becoming veil, predominantly white, adjusted to her countenance; which through it somehow, even to his imperfect sight, showed strong fine black brows and what he would have called on the spot character. But she was pale; her black brows were the blacker behind the flattering tissue; she still kept a hand, for support, on the terrace-rail, while the other, at the end of an extended arm that had an effect of rigidity, clearly pressed hard on the knob of a small and shining umbrella, the lower extremity of whose stick was equally, was sustainingly, firm on the walk. So this mature, qualified, important person stood and looked at the limp, undistinguished—oh his values of aspect now!— shabby man on the bench.

It was extraordinary, but the fact of her interest, by immensely surprising, by immediately agitating him, blinded him at first to her identity and, for the space of his long stare, diverted him from it; with which even then, when recognition did break, the sense of the shock, striking inward, simply consumed itself in gaping stillness. He sat there motionless and weak, fairly faint with surprise, and there was no instant, in all the succession of so many, at which Kate Cookham could have caught the special sign of his intelligence. Yet that she did catch something he saw—for he saw her steady herself, by her two supported hands, to meet it; while, after she had done so, a very wonderful thing happened, of which he could scarce, later on, have made a clear statement, though he was to think it over again and again. She moved toward him, she reached him, she stood there, she sat down near him, he merely passive and wonderstruck, unresentfully "impressed," gaping and taking it in—and all as with an open allowance on the part of each, so that they positively and quite intimately met in it, o the impertinence for their case, this case that brought them again, after horrible years, face to face, of the vanity, the profanity, the impossibility, of anything between them but silence.

Nearer to him, beside him at a considerable interval (oh she was immensely considerate!) she presented him, in the sharp terms of her transformed state—but thus the more amply, formally, ceremoniously—with the reasons that would serve him best for not having precipitately known her. She was simply another and a totally different person, and the exhibition of it to which she had proceeded with this solemn anxiety was all, obviously, for his benefit—once he had, as he appeared to be doing, provisionally accepted her approach. He had remembered her as inclined to the massive and disowned by the graceful; but this was a spare, fine, worn, almost wasted lady—who had repaired waste, it was true, however, with something he could only appreciate as a rich accumulation of manner. She was strangely older, so far as that went—marked by experience and as if many things had happened to her; her face had suffered, to its improvement, contraction and concentration; and if he had granted, of old and from the first, that her eyes were remarkable, had they yet ever had for him this sombre glow? Withal, something said, she had flourished—he felt it, wincing at it, as that; she had had a life, a career, a history—something that her present waiting air and nervous consciousness couldn't prevent his noting there as a deeply latent assurance. She had flourished, she had flourished—though to learn it after this fashion was somehow at the same time not to feel she flaunted it. It wasn't thus execration that she revived in him; she made in fact, exhibitively, as he could only have put it, the matter of long ago irrelevant, and these extraordinary minutes of their reconstituted relation—how many? how few?—addressed themselves altogether to new possibilities.

Still it after a little awoke in him as with the throb of a touched nerve that his own very attitude was supplying a connection; he knew presently that he wouldn't have had her go, *couldn't* have made a sign to her for it—which was what she had been uncertain of—without speaking to him; and that therefore he was, as at the other, the hideous time, passive to whatever she might do. She was even yet, she was always, in possession of him; she had known how and where to find him and had appointed that he should see her, and, though he had never dreamed it was again to happen to him, he was meeting it already as if it might have been the only thing that the least humanly *could*. Yes, he had come back there to flop, by long custom, upon the bench of desolation *as* the man in the whole place, precisely, to whom nothing worth more than tuppence could happen; whereupon, in the grey desert of his consciousness, the very earth had suddenly opened and flamed. With this, further, it came over him that he hadn't been prepared and that his wretched appearance must show it. He wasn't fit to receive a visit—any visit; a flush for his felt misery, in the light of her opulence, broke out in his lean cheeks. But if he coloured he sat as he was—she should at least, as a visitor, be satisfied. His eyes only, at last, turned from her and resumed a little their gaze at the sea. That, however, didn't relieve him, and he perpetrated in the course of another moment the odd desperate gesture of raising both his hands to his face and letting them, while he pressed it to them, cover and guard it. It was as he held them there that she at last spoke.

"I'll go away if you wish me to." And then she waited a moment. "I mean now—now that you've seen I'm here. I wanted you to know it, and I thought of writing—I was afraid of our meeting accidentally. Then I was afraid that if I wrote you might refuse. So I thought of this way—as I knew you must come out here." She went on with pauses, giving him a chance to make a sign. "I've waited several days. But I'll do what you wish. Only I should like in that case to come back." Again she stopped; but strange was it to him that he wouldn't have made her break off. She held him in boundless wonder. "I came down—I mean I came from town—on purpose. I'm staying on still, and I've a great patience and will give you time. Only may I say it's important? Now that I do see you," she brought out in the same way, "I see how inevitable it was—I mean that I should have wanted to come. But you must feel about it as you can," she wound up—"till you get used to the idea."

She spoke so for accommodation, for discretion, for some ulterior view already expressed in her manner, that, after taking well in, from behind his hands, that this was her very voice—oh ladylike!—heard, and heard in deprecation of displeasure, after long years again, he uncovered his face and freshly met her eyes. More than ever he couldn't have known her. Less and less remained of the figure all the facts of which had long ago so hardened for him. She was a handsome, grave, authoritative, but refined and, as it were, physically rearranged person—she, the outrageous vulgarity of whose prime assault had kept him shuddering so long as a shudder was in him. That atrocity in her was what everything had been built on, but somehow, all strangely, it was slipping from him; so that, after the oddest fashion conceivable, when he felt he mustn't let her go, it was as if he were putting out his hand to save the past, the hideous real unalterable past, exactly as she had been the cause of its being and the cause of his undergoing it. He should have been too awfully "sold" if he wasn't going to have been right about her.

"I don't mind," he heard himself at last say. Not to mind seemed for the instant the length he was prepared to go; but he was afterward aware of how soon he must have added: "You've come on purpose to see me?" He was on the point of putting to her further: "What then do you want of me?" But he would keep—yes, in time—from appearing to show he cared. If he showed he cared, where then would be his revenge? So he was already, within five minutes, thinking his revenge uncomfortably over instead of just comfortably knowing it. What came to him, at any rate, as they actually fell to talk, was that, with such precautions, considerations, reduplications of consciousness, almost avowed feelings of her way on her own part, and light fingerings of his chords of sensibility, she was understanding, she *had* understood, more things than all the years, up to this strange eventide, had given him an inkling of. They talked, they went on—he hadn't let her retreat, to whatever it committed him and however abjectly it did so; yet keeping off and off, dealing with such surface facts as involved ancient acquaintance but held abominations at bay. The recognition, the attestation that she *had* come down for him, that there would be reasons, that she had even hovered and watched, assured herself a little of his habits (which she managed to speak of as if, on their present ampler development, they were much to be deferred to), detained them enough to make vivid how, listen as stiffly or as serenely as he might, she sat there in fear, just as she had so stood there at first, and that her fear had really to do with her calculation of some sort of chance with him. What chance could it possibly be? Whatever it might have done, on this prodigious showing, with Kate Cookham, it made the present witness to the state of his fortunes simply exquisite: he ground his teeth secretly together as he saw he should have to take *that*. For what did it mean but that she would have liked to pity him if she could have done it with safety? Ah, however, he must give her no measure of safety!

By the time he had remarked, with that idea, that she probably saw few changes about them there that weren't for the worse—the place was going down, down and down, so fast that goodness knew where it would stop—and had also mentioned that in spite of this he himself remained faithful, with all its faults loving it still; by the time he had, after that fashion, superficially indulged her, adding a few further light and just sufficiently dry reflections on local matters, the disappearance of landmarks and important persons, the frequency of gales, the low policy of the town-council in playing down to cheap excursionists: by the time he had so acquitted himself, and she had observed, of her own motion, that she was staying at the Royal, which he knew for the time-honoured, the conservative and exclusive hotel, he had made out for himself one thing at least, the amazing fact that he had been landed by his troubles, at the end of time, in a "social relation," of all things in the world, and how of that luxury he was now having unprecedented experience. He had but once in his life had his nose in the Royal, on the occasion of his himself delivering a parcel during some hiatus in his succession of impossible small boys and meeting in the hall the lady who had bought of him, in the morning, a set of Crabbe, largely, he flattered himself, under the artful persuasion of his acute remarks on that author, gracefully associated by him, in this colloquy, he remembered, with a glance at Charles Lamb as well, and who went off in a day or two without settling, though he received her cheque from London three or four months later.

That hadn't been a social relation; and truly, deep within his appeal to himself to be remarkable, to be imperturbable and impenetrable, to be in fact quite incomparable now, throbbed the intense vision of his drawing out and draining dry the sensation he had begun to taste. He would do it, moreover—that would be the refinement of his art—not only without the betraying anxiety of a single question, but just even by seeing her flounder (since she must, in a vagueness deeply disconcerting to her) as to her real effect on him. She was distinctly floundering by the time he had brought her—it had taken ten minutes—down to a consciousness of absurd and twaddling topics, to the reported precarious state, for instance, of the syndicate running the Bijou Theatre at the Pierhead—all as an admonition that she might want him to want to know why she was thus waiting on him, might want it for all she was worth, before he had ceased to be so remarkable as not to ask her. He didn't—and this assuredly was wondrous enough—want to do anything worse to her than let her flounder; but he was willing to do that so long as it mightn't prevent his seeing at least where *he* was. He seemed still to see where he was even at the minute that followed her final break-off, clearly intended to be resolute, from make-believe talk.

"I wonder if I might prevail on you to come to tea with me to-morrow at five."

He didn't so much as answer it—though he could scarcely believe his ears. To-morrow was Sunday, and the proposal referred, clearly, to the custom of "five-o'clock" tea, known to him only by the contemporary novel of manners and the catchy advertisement of table-linen. He had never in his life been present at any such luxurious rite, but he was offering practical indifference to it as a false mark of his sense that his social relation had already risen to his chin. "I gave up my very modest, but rather interesting little old book business, perhaps you know, ever so long ago."

She floundered so that she could say nothing—meet *that* with no possible word; all the less too that his tone, casual and colourless, wholly defied any apprehension of it as a reverse. Silence only came; but after a moment she returned to her effort. "If you *can* come I shall be at home. To see you otherwise than thus was in fact what, as I tell you, I came down for. But I leave it," she returned, "to your feeling."

He had at this, it struck him, an inspiration; which he required however a minute or two to decide to carry out; a minute or two during which the shake of his foot over his knee became an intensity of fidget. "Of course I know I still owe you a large sum of money. If it's about *that* you wish to see me," he went on, "I may as well tell you just here that I shall be able to meet my full obligation in the future as little as I've met it in the past. I can never," said Herbert Dodd, "pay up that balance."

He had looked at her while he spoke, but on finishing looked off at the sea again and continued to agitate his foot. He knew now what he had done and why; and the sense of her fixed dark eyes on him during his speech and after didn't alter his small contentment. Yet even when she still said nothing he didn't turn round; he simply kept his corner as if *that* were his point made, should it even be the last word between them. It might have been, for that matter, from the way in which she presently rose, gathering herself, her fine umbrella and her very small smart reticule, in the cons-truction of which shining gilt much figured, well together, and, after standing another instant, moved across to the rail of the terrace as she had done before and remained, as before, with her back to him, though this time, it well might be, under a different fear. A quarter of an hour ago she hadn't tried him, and had had that anxiety; now that she had tried him it wasn't easier—but she was thinking what she still could do. He left her to think—nothing in fact more interesting than the way she might decide had ever happened to him; but it was a part of this also that as she turned round and came nearer again he didn't rise, he gave her no help. If she got any, at least, from his looking up at her only, meeting her fixed eyes once more in silence, that was her own affair. "You must think," she said—"you must take all your time, but I shall be at home." She left it to him thus—she insisted, with her idea, on leaving him something too. And on her side as well she showed an art—which resulted, after another instant, in his having to rise to his feet. He flushed afresh as he did it—it exposed him so shabbily the more; and now if she took him in, with each of his seedy items, from head to foot, he didn't and couldn't and wouldn't know it, attaching his eyes hard and straight to something quite away from them.

It stuck in his throat to say he'd come, but she had so curious a way with her that he still less could say he wouldn't, and in a moment had taken refuge in something that was neither. "Are you married?"—he put it to her with that plainness, though it had seemed before he said it to do more for him than while she waited before replying.

"No, I'm not married," she said; and then had another wait that might have amounted to a question of what this had to do with it.

He surely couldn't have told her; so that he had recourse, a little poorly as he felt, but to an "Oh!" that still left them opposed. He turned away for it—that is for the poorness, which, lingering in the air, had almost a vulgar platitude; and when he presently again wheeled about she had fallen off as for quitting him, only with a pause, once more, for a last look. It was all a bit awkward, but he had another happy thought, which consisted in his silently raising his hat as for a sign of dignified dismissal. He had cultivated of old, for the occasions of life, the right, the discriminated bow, and now, out of the grey limbo of the time when he could care for such things, this flicker of propriety leaped and worked She might, for that matter, herself have liked it; since, receding further, only with her white face toward him, she paid it the homage of submission. He remained dignified, and she almost humbly went.

V

Nothing in the world, on the Sunday afternoon, could have prevented him from going; he was not after all destitute of three or four such articles of clothing as, if they wouldn't particularly grace the occasion, wouldn't positively dishonour it. That deficiency might have kept him away, but no voice of the spirit, no consideration of pride. It sweetened his impatience in fact—for he fairly felt it a long time to wait—that his pride would really most find its account in his acceptance of these conciliatory steps. From the moment he could put it in that way—that he couldn't refuse to hear what she might have, so very elaborately, to say for herself—he ought certainly to be at his ease; in illustration of which he whistled odd snatches to himself as he hung about on that cloud-dappled autumn Sunday, a mild private minstrelsy that his lips hadn't known since when? The interval of the twenty-four hours, made longer by a night of many more revivals than oblivions, had in fact dragged not a little; in spite of which, however, our extremely brushed-up and trimmed and polished friend knew an unprecedented flutter as he was ushered, at the Royal Hotel, into Miss Cookham's sitting-room. Yes, it was an adventure, and he had never had an adventure in his life; the term, for him, was essentially a term of high appreciation—such as disqualified for that figure, under due criticism, every single passage of his past career.

What struck him at the moment as qualifying in the highest degree this actual passage was the fact that at no great distance from his hostess in the luxurious room, as he apprehended it, in which the close of day had begun to hang a few shadows, sat a gentleman who rose as she rose, and whose name she at once mentioned to him. He had for Herbert Dodd all the air of a swell, the gentleman—rather red-faced and bald-headed, but moustachioed, waistcoated, necktied to the highest pitch, with an effect of chains and rings, of shining teeth in a glassily monocular smile; a wondrous apparition to have been asked to "meet" him, as in contemporary fiction, or for him to have been asked to meet. "Captain Roper, Mr. Herbert Dodd"— their entertainer introduced them, yes; but with a sequel immediately afterward more disconcerting apparently to Captain Roper himself even than to her second and more breathless visitor; a "Well then, good-bye till the next time," with a hand thrust straight out, which allowed the personage so addressed no alternative but to lay aside his teacup, even though Herbert saw there was a good deal left in it, and glare about him for his hat. Miss Cookham had had her tea-tray on a small table before her, she had served Captain Roper while waiting for Mr. Dodd; but she simply dismissed him now, with a high sweet unmistakable decision, a knowledge of what she was about, as our hero would have called it, which enlarged at a stroke the latter's view of the number of different things and sorts of things, in the sphere of the manners and ways of those living at their ease, that a social relation would put before one. Captain Roper would have liked to remain, would have liked more tea, but Kate signified in this direct fashion that she had had enough of him. Herbert had seen things, in his walk of life—rough things, plenty; but never things smoothed with that especial smoothness, carried out as it were by the fine form of Captain Roper's own retreat, which included even a bright convulsed leave-taking cognisance of the plain, vague individual, of no lustre at all and with the very low-class guard of an old silver watch buttoned away under an ill-made coat, to whom he was sacrificed.

It came to Herbert as he left the place a shade less remarkable—though there was still wonder enough and to spare—that he had been even publicly and designedly sacrificed; exactly so that, as the door closed behind him, Kate Cookham, standing there to wait for it, could seem to say, across the room, to the friend of her youth, only by the expression of her fine eyes: "There—see what I do for you!" "For" him—that was the extraordinary thing, and not less so that he was already, within three minutes, after this fashion, taking it in as by the intensity of a new light; a light that was one somehow with this rich inner air of the plush-draped and much-mirrored hotel, where the fire-glow and the approach of evening confirmed together the privacy, and the loose curtains at the wide window were parted for a command of his old lifelong Parade—the field of life so familiar to him from below and in the wind and the wet, but which he had never in all the long years hung over at this vantage.

"He's an acquaintance, but a bore," his hostess explained in respect to Captain Roper. "He turned up yesterday, but I didn't invite him, and I had said to him before you came in that I was expecting a gentleman with whom I should wish to be alone. I go quite straight at my idea that way, as a rule; but you know," she now strikingly went on, "how straight I go. And he had had," she added, "his tea."

Dodd had been looking all round—had taken in, with the rest, the brightness, the distinguished elegance, as he supposed it, of the tea-service with which she was dealing and the variously tinted appeal of certain savoury edibles on plates. "Oh but he *hadn't* had his tea!" he heard himself the next moment earnestly reply; which speech had at once betrayed, he was then quickly aware, the candour of his interest, the unsophisticated state that had survived so many troubles. If he was so interested how could he be proud, and if he was proud how could he be so interested?

He had made her at any rate laugh outright, and was further conscious, for this, both that it was the first time of that since their new meeting, and that it didn't affect him as harsh. It affected him, however, as free, for she replied at once, still smiling and as a part of it: "Oh, I think we shall get on!"

This told him he had made some difference for her, shown her the way, or something like it, that she hadn't been sure of yesterday; which moreover wasn't what he had intended—he had come armed for showing her nothing; so that after she had gone on with the same gain of gaiety, "You must at any rate comfortably have yours," there was but one answer for him to make.

His eyes played again over the tea-things—they seemed strangely to help him; but he didn't sit down.

"I've come, as you see—but I've come, please, to understand; and if you require to be alone with me, and if I break bread with you, it seems to me I should first know exactly where I am and to what you suppose I so commit myself." He had thought it out and over and over, particularly the turn about breaking bread; though perhaps he didn't give it, in her presence—this was impossible, her presence altered so many things—quite the full sound or the weight he had planned.

But it had none the less come to his aid—it had made her perfectly grave. "You commit yourself to nothing. You're perfectly free. It's only I who commit myself."

On which, while she stood there as if all handsomely and deferentially waiting for him to consider and decide, he would have been naturally moved to ask her what she committed herself then *to*—so moved, that is, if he hadn't, before saying it, thought more sharply still of something better. "Oh, that's another thing."

"Yes, that's another thing," Kate Cookham returned. To which she added, "So *now* won't you sit down?" He sank with deliberation into the seat from which Captain Roper had risen; she went back to her own and while she did so spoke again. "I'm *not* free. At least," she said over her tea-tray, "I'm free only for this."

Everything was there before them and around them, everything massive and shining, so that he had instinctively fallen back in his chair as for the wondering, the resigned acceptance of it; where her last words stirred in him a sense of odd deprecation. Only for "that"? "That" was everything, at this moment, to his long inanition, and the effect, as if she had suddenly and perversely mocked him, was to press the spring of a protest. "Isn't 'this' then riches?"

"Riches?" she smiled over, handing him his cup—for she had triumphed in having struck from him a question.

"I mean haven't you a lot of money?" He didn't care now that it was out; his cup was in his hand, and what was that but proved interest? He had succumbed to the social relation.

"Yes, I've money. Of course you wonder—but I've wanted you to wonder. It was to make you take that in that I came. So now you know," she said, leaning back where she faced him, but in a straighter chair and with her arms closely folded, after a fashion characteristic of her, as for some control of her nerves.

"You came to show you've money?"

"That's one of the things. Not a lot—not even very much. But enough," said Kate Cookham.

"Enough? I should think so!" he again couldn't help a bit crudely exhaling.

"Enough for what I wanted. I don't always live like this—not at all. But I came to the best hotel on purpose. I wanted to show you I could. Now," she asked, "do you understand?"

"Understand?" He only gaped.

She threw up her loosed arms, which dropped again beside her. "I did it *for* you—I did it *for* you!"

"'For' me—?"

"What I did—what I did here of old."

He stared, trying to see it. "When you made me pay you?"

"The Two Hundred and Seventy—all I could get from you, as you reminded me yesterday, so that I had to give up the rest It was my idea," she went on—"it was my idea."

"To bleed me quite to death?" Oh, his ice was broken now!

"To make you raise money—since you could, you *could*. You did, you did—so what better proof?"

His hands fell from what he had touched; he could only stare—her own manner for it was different now too. "I did. I did indeed—!" And the woful weak simplicity of it, which seemed somehow all that was left him, fell even on his own ear.

"Well then, here it is—it isn't lost!" she returned with a graver face.

"'Here' it is," he gasped, "my poor agonised old money—my blood?"

"Oh, it's *my* blood too, you must know now!" She held up

her head as not before—as for her right to speak of the thing to-day most precious to her. "I took it, but this—my being here this way—is what I've made of it! That was the idea I had!"

Her "ideas," as things to boast of, staggered him. "To have everything in the world, like this, at my wretched expense?"

She had folded her arms back again—grasping each elbow she sat firm; she knew he could see, and had known well from the first, what she had wanted to say, difficult, monstrous though it might be. "No more than at my own— but to do something with your money that you'd never do yourself."

"Myself, myself?" he wonderingly wailed. "Do you know— or don't you?—what my life has been?"

She waited, and for an instant, though the light in the room had failed a little more and would soon be mainly that of the flaring lamps on the windy Parade, he caught from her dark eye a silver gleam of impatience. "You've suffered and you've worked—which, God knows, is what I've done! *Of course* you've suffered," she said—"you inevitably had to! We have to," she went on, "to do or to be or to get anything."

"And pray what have I done or been or got?" Herbert Dodd found it almost desolately natural to demand.

It made her cover him again as with all she was thinking of. "Can you imagine nothing, or can't you conceive—?" And then as her challenge struck deeper in, deeper down than it had yet reached, and with the effect of a rush of the blood to his face, "It was *for* you, it was *for* you!" she again broke out—"and for what or whom else could it have been?"

He saw things to a tune now that made him answer straight: "I thought at one time it might be for Bill Frankle."

"Yes—that was the way you treated me," Miss Cookham as plainly replied.

But he let this pass; his thought had already got away from it. "What good then—its having been for me—has that ever done me?"

"Doesn't it do you any good *now?*" his friend returned. To which she added, with another dim play of her tormented brightness, before he could speak: "But if you won't even have your tea—!"

He had in fact touched nothing and, if he could have explained, would have pleaded very veraciously that his appetite, keen when he came in, had somehow suddenly failed. It was beyond eating or drinking, what she seemed to want him to take from her. So if he looked, before him, over the array, it was to say, very grave and graceless: "Am I to understand that you offer to repay me?"

"I offer to repay you with interest, Herbert Dodd"—and her emphasis of the great word was wonderful.

It held him in his place a minute, and held his eyes upon her; after which, agitated too sharply to sit still, he pushed back his chair and stood up. It was as if mere distress or dismay at first worked in him, and was in fact a wave of deep and irresistible emotion which made him, on his feet, sway as in a great trouble and then, to correct it, throw himself stiffly toward the window, where he stood and looked out unseeing. The road, the wide terrace beyond, the seats, the eternal sea beyond that, the lighted lamps now flaring in the October night-wind, with the few dispersed people abroad at the tea-hour; these things, meeting and melting into the firelit hospitality at his elbow—or was it that portentous amenity that melted into *them?*—seemed to form round him and to put before him, all together, the strangest of circles and the newest of experiences, in which the unforgettable and the unimaginable were confoundingly mixed. "Oh, oh, oh!"—he could only almost howl for it.

And then, while a thick blur for some moments mantled everything, he knew she had got up, that she stood watching him, allowing for everything, again all "cleverly" patient with him, and he heard her speak again as with studied quietness and clearness. "I wanted to take care of you—it was what I first wanted—and what you first consented to. I'd have done it, oh I'd have done it, I'd have loved you and helped you and guarded you, and you'd have had no trouble, no bad blighting ruin, in all your easy, yes, just your quite jolly and comfortable life. I showed you and proved to you this—I brought it home to you, as I fondly fancied, and it made me briefly happy. You swore you cared for me, you wrote it and made me believe it—you pledged me your honour and your faith. Then you turned and changed suddenly from one day to another; everything altered, you broke your vows, you as good as told me you only wanted it off. You faced me with dislike, and in fact tried not to face me at all; you behaved as if you hated me—you had seen a girl, of great beauty, I admit, who made me a fright and a bore."

This brought him straight round. "No, Kate Cookham."

"Yes, Herbert Dodd." She but shook her head, calmly and nobly, in the now gathered dusk, and her memories and her cause and her character—or was it only her arch-subtlety, her line and her "idea"?—gave her an extraordinary large assurance.

She had touched, however, the treasure of his own case—his terrible own case that began to live again at once by the force of her talking of hers, and which could always all cluster about his great asseveration. "No, no, never, never; I had never seen her then and didn't dream of her; so that when you yourself began to be harsh and sharp with me, and to seem to want to quarrel, I could have but one idea—which was an appearance you didn't in the least, as I saw it then, account for or disprove."

"An appearance—?" Kate desired, as with high astonishment, to know which one.

"How *shouldn't* I have supposed you really to care for Bill Frankle?—as thoroughly believing the motive of your claim for my money to be its help to your marrying him, since you couldn't marry me. I was only surprised when, time passing, I made out that that hadn't happened; and perhaps," he added the next instant with something of a conscious lapse from the finer style, "hadn't been in question."

She had listened to this only staring, and she was silent after he had said it, so silent for some instants that while he considered her something seemed to fail him, much as if he had thrown out his foot for a step and not found the place to rest it. He jerked round to the window again, and then she answered, but without passion unless it was that of her weariness for something stupid and forgiven in him, "Oh, the blind, the pitiful folly!"—to which, as it might perfectly have applied to her own behaviour, he returned nothing. She had moreover at once gone on. "Have it then that there wasn't much to do—between your finding that you loathed me for another woman or discovering only, when it came to the point, that you loathed me quite enough for myself."

Which, as she put it in that immensely effective fashion, he recognised that he must just unprotestingly and not so very awkwardly—not so *very!*—take from her; since, whatever he had thus come to her for, it wasn't to perjure himself with any pretence that, "another woman" or no other woman, he hadn't, for years and years, abhorred her. Now he was taking tea with her—or rather, literally, seemed not to be; but this made no difference, and he let her express it as she would while he distinguished a man he knew, Charley Coote, outside on the Parade, under favour of the empty hour and one of the flaring lamps, making up to a young woman with whom (it stuck out grotesquely in his manner) he had never before conversed. Dodd's own position was that of acquiescing in this recall of what had so bitterly been—but he hadn't come back to her, of himself, to stir up, to recall or to recriminate, and for *her* it could but be the very lesson of her whole present act that if she touched anything she touched everything. Soon enough she *was* indeed, and all overwhelmingly, touching everything—with a hand of which the boldness grew.

"But I didn't let *that,* even, make a difference in what I wanted—which was all," she said, "and had only and passionately been, to take care of you. I had *no* money whatever—nothing then of my own, not a penny to come by anyhow; so it wasn't with mine I could do it. But I could do it with yours," she amazingly wound up—"if I could once get yours out of you."

He faced straight about again—his eyebrows higher than they had ever been in his life. "Mine? What penny of it was mine? What scrap beyond a bare, mean little living had I ever pretended to have?"

She held herself still a minute, visibly with force; only her eyes consciously attached to the seat of a chair the back of which her hands, making it tilt toward her a little, grasped as for support. "You pretended to have enough to marry me—and that was all I afterward claimed of you when you wouldn't."

He was on the point of retorting that he had absolutely pretended to nothing—least of all to the primary desire that such a way of stating it fastened on him; he was on the point for ten seconds of giving her full in the face: "I never *had* any such dream till you yourself—infatuated with me as, frankly, you on the whole appeared to be—got round me and muddled me up and made me behave as if in a way that went against the evidence of my senses." But he was to feel as quickly that, whatever the ugly, the spent, the irrecoverable truth, he might better have bitten his tongue off: there beat on him there this strange and other, this so prodigiously different beautiful and dreadful truth that no far remembrance and no abiding ache of his own could wholly falsify, and that was indeed all out with her next words. "That—*using* it for you and using you yourself for your own future—was my motive. I've led my life, which has been an affair, I assure you; and, as I've told you without your quite seeming to understand, I've brought everything fivefold back to you."

The perspiration broke out on his forehead. "Everything's mine?" he quavered as for the deep piercing pain of it.

"Everything!" said Kate Cookham.

So it told him how she had loved him—but with the tremendous effect at once of its only glaring out at him from the whole thing that it was verily she, a thousand times over, who, in the exposure of his youth and his vanity, had, on the bench of desolation, the scene of yesterday's own renewal, left for him no forward steps to take. It hung there for him tragically vivid again, the hour she had first found him sequestered and accessible after making his acquaintance at his shop. And from this, by a succession of links that fairly clicked to his ear as with their perfect fitting, the fate and the pain and the payment of others stood together in a great grim order. Everything there then was *his*—to make him ask what had been Nan's, poor Nan's of the constant question of whether he need have collapsed. She was before him, she was between them, his little dead dissatisfied wife; across all whose final woe and whose lowly grave he was to reach out, it appeared, to take gifts. He saw them too, the gifts; saw them—she bristled with them—in his actual companion's brave and sincere and authoritative figure, her strangest of demonstrations. But the other appearance was intenser, as if their ghost had waved wild arms; so that half a minute hadn't passed before the one poor thing that remained of Nan, and that yet thus became a quite mighty and momentous poor thing, was sitting on his lips as for its sole opportunity.

"Can you give me your word of honour that I mightn't, under decent advice, have defied you?"

It made her turn very white; but now that she had said what she *had* said she could still hold up her head. "Certainly you might have defied me, Herbert Dodd."

"They would have told me you had no legal case?"

Well, if she was pale she was bold. "You talk of decent advice—!" She broke off, there was too much to say, and all needless. What she said instead was: "They would have told you I had nothing."

"I didn't so much as ask," her sad visitor remarked.

"Of course you didn't so much as ask."

"I couldn't be so outrageously vulgar," he went on.

"*I* could, by God's help!" said Kate Cookham.

"Thank you." He had found at his command a tone that made him feel more gentlemanlike than he had ever felt in his life or should doubtless ever feel again. It might have been enough—but somehow as they stood there with this immense clearance between them it wasn't. The clearance was like a sudden gap or great bleak opening through which there blew upon them a deadly chill. Too many things had fallen away, too many new rolled up and over him, and they made something within shake him to his base. It upset the full vessel, and though she kept her eyes on him he let that consequence come, bursting into tears, weakly crying there before her even as he had cried to himself in the hour of his youth when she had made him groundlessly fear. She turned away then—*that* she couldn't watch, and had presently flung herself on the sofa and, all responsively wailing, buried her own face on the cushioned arm. So for a minute their smothered sobs only filled the room. But he made out, through this disorder, where he had put down his hat; his stick and his new tan-coloured gloves—they had cost two-and-thruppence and would have represented sacrifices—were on the chair beside it He picked these articles up and all silently and softly—gasping, that is, but quite on tiptoe—reached the door and let himself out.

VI

Off there on the bench of desolation a week later she made him a more particular statement, which it had taken the remarkably tense interval to render possible. After leaving her at the hotel that last Sunday he had gone forth in his reaggravated trouble and walked straight before him, in the teeth of the west wind, close to the iron rails of the stretched Marina and with his telltale face turned from persons occasionally met, and toward the surging sea. At the Land's End, even in the confirmed darkness and the perhaps imminent big blow, his immemorial nook, small shelter as it yielded, had again received him; and it was in the course of this heedless session, no doubt, where the agitated air had nothing to add to the commotion within him, that he began to look his extraordinary fortune a bit straighter in the face and see it confess itself at once a fairy-tale and a nightmare That, visibly, confoundingly, she was still attached to him (attached in fact was a mild word!) and that the unquestionable proof of it was in this offered pecuniary salve, of the thickest composition, for his wounds and sores and shames—these things were the fantastic fable, the tale of money in handfuls, that he seemed to have only to stand there and swallow and digest and feel himself full-fed by; but the whole of the rest was nightmare, and most of all nightmare his having thus to thank one through whom Nan and his little girls had known torture.

He didn't care for himself now, and this unextinguished and apparently inextinguishable charm by which he had held her was a fact incredibly romantic; but he gazed with a longer face than he had ever had for anything in the world at his potential acceptance of a great bouncing benefit from the person he intimately, if even in a manner indirectly, associated with the conditions to which his lovely wife and his children (who would have been so lovely too) had pitifully succumbed. He had accepted the social relation—which meant he had taken even that on trial—without knowing what it so dazzlingly masked; for a social relation it had become with a vengeance when it drove him about the place as now at his hours of freedom (and he actually and recklessly took, all demoralised and unstrung and unfit either for work or for anything else, other liberties that would get him into trouble) under this queer torment of irreconcilable things, a bewildered consciousness of tenderness and patience and cruelty, of great evident mystifying facts that were as little to be questioned as to be conceived or explained, and that were yet least, withal, to be lost sight of.

On that Sunday night he had wandered wild, incoherently ranging and throbbing, but this became the law of his next days as well, since he lacked more than ever all other resort or refuge and had nowhere to carry, to deposit, or contractedly let loose and lock up, as it were, his swollen consciousness, which fairly split in twain the raw shell of his sordid little boarding-place. The arch of the sky and the spread of sea and shore alone gave him space; he could roam with himself anywhere, in short, far or near—he could only never take himself back. That certitude—that this was impossible to him even should she wait there among her plushes and bronzes ten years—was the thing he kept closest clutch of; it did wonders for what he would have called his self-respect. Exactly as he had left her so he would stand off—even though at moments when he pulled up sharp somewhere to put himself an intensest question his heart almost stood still. The days of the week went by, and as he had left her she stayed; to the extent, that is, of his having neither sight nor sound of her, and of the failure of every sign. It took nerve, he said, not to return to her, even for curiosity—since how, after all, in the name of wonder, had she invested the fruits of her extortion to such advantage, there being no chapter of all the obscurity of the years to beat that for queer-ness? But he dropped, tired to death, on benches, half a dozen times an evening—exactly on purpose to recognise that the nerve required was just the nerve he had.

As the days without a token from her multiplied he came in as well for hours—and these indeed mainly on the bench of desolation—of sitting stiff and stark in presence of the probability that he had lost everything for ever. When he passed the Royal he never turned an eyelash, and when he met Captain Roper on the Front, three days after having been introduced to him, he "cut him dead"—another privileged consequence of a social relation—rather than seem to himself to make the remotest approach to the question of whether Miss Cookham had left Properley. He had cut people in the days of his life before, just as he had come to being himself cut—since there had been no time for him wholly without one or other face of that necessity—but had never effected such a severance as of this rare connection, which helped to give him thus the measure of his really precious sincerity. If he had lost what had hovered before him he had lost it, his only tribute to which proposition was to grind his teeth with one of those "scrunches," as he would have said, of which the violence fairly reached his ear. It wouldn't make him lift a finger, and in fact if Kate had simply taken herself off on the Tuesday or the Wednesday she would have been reabsorbed again into the darkness from which she had emerged—and no lifting of fingers, the unspeakable chapter closed, would evermore avail. That at any rate was the kind of man he still was—even after all that had come and gone, and even if for a few dazed hours certain things had seemed pleasant. The dazed hours had passed, the surge of the old bitterness had dished him (shouldn't he have been shamed if it hadn't?), and he might sit there as before, as always, with nothing at all on earth to look to. He had therefore wrongfully believed himself to be degraded; and the last word about him would be that he *couldn't* then, it appeared, sink to vulgarity as he had tried to let his miseries make him.

And yet on the next Sunday morning, face to face with him again at the Land's End, what she very soon came to was: "As if I believed you didn't *know* by what cord you hold me!" Absolutely too, and just that morning in fact, above all, he wouldn't, he quite couldn't have taken his solemn oath that he hadn't a sneaking remnant, as he might have put it to himself—a remnant of faith in tremendous things still to come of their interview. The day was sunny and breezy, the sea of a cold purple; he wouldn't go to church as he mostly went of Sunday mornings, that being in its way too a social relation—and not least when two-and-thruppenny tan-coloured gloves were new; which indeed he had the art of keeping them for ages. Yet he would dress himself as he scarce mustered resources for even to figure on the fringe of Society, local and transient, at St. Bernard's, and in this trim he took his way westward; occupied largely, as he went, it might have seemed to any person pursuing the same course and happening to observe him, in a fascinated study of the motions of his shadow, the more or less grotesque shape projected, in front of him and mostly a bit to the right, over the blanched asphalt of the Parade and dandling and dancing at such a rate, shooting out and then contracting, that, viewed in themselves, its eccentricities might have formed the basis of an interesting challenge: "Find the state of mind, guess the nature of the agitation, possessing the person so remarkably represented!" Herbert Dodd, for that matter, might have been himself attempting to make by the sun's sharp aid some approach to his immediate horoscope.

It had at any rate been thus put before him that the dandling and dancing of his image occasionally gave way to perfect immobility, when he stopped and kept his eyes on it. "Suppose she should come, suppose she *should!*" it is revealed at least to ourselves that he had at these moments audibly breathed—breathed with the intensity of an arrest between hope and fear. It had glimmered upon him from early, with the look of the day, that, given all else that could happen, this would be rather, as he put it, in her line; and the possibility lived for him, as he proceeded, to the tune of a suspense almost sickening. It was, from one small stage of his pilgrimage to another, the "For ever, never!" of the sentimental case the playmates of his youth used to pretend to settle by plucking the petals of a daisy. But it came to his truly turning faint—so "queer" he felt—when, at the gained point of the long stretch from which he could always tell, he arrived within positive sight of his immemorial goal. His seat was taken and she was keeping it for him—it could only be *she* there in possession; whereby it shone out for Herbert Dodd that if he hadn't been quite sure of her recurrence she had at least been quite sure of his. *That* pulled him up to some purpose, where recognition began for them—or to the effect, in other words, of his pausing to judge if he could bear, for the sharpest note of their intercourse, this inveterate demonstration of her making him do what she liked. What settled the question for him then—and just while they avowedly watched each other, over the long interval, before closing, as if, on either side, for the major advantage—what settled it was this very fact that what she liked she liked so terribly. If it were simply to "use" him, as she had said the last time, and no matter to the profit of which of them she called it, one might let it go for that; since it could make her wait over, day after day, in that fashion, and with such a spending of money, on the hazard of their meeting again. How could she be the least sure he would ever again consent to it after the proved action on him, a week ago, of her last monstrous honesty? It was indeed positively as if he were now himself putting this influence—and for their common edification—to the supreme, to the finest test. He had a sublime, an ideal flight, which lasted about a minute. "Suppose, now that I see her there and what she has taken so characteristically for granted, suppose I just show her that she *hasn't* only confidently to wait or whistle for me, and that the length of my leash is greater than she measures, and that everything's impossible always?—show it by turning my back on her now and walking straight away. She won't be able not to understand *that!*"

Nothing had passed, across their distance, but the mute apprehension of each on the part of each; the whole expanse, at the church hour, was void of other life (he had scarce met a creature on his way from end to end), and the sun-seasoned gusts kept brushing the air and all the larger prospect clean. It was through this beautiful lucidity that he watched her watch him, as it were—watch him for what he would do. Neither moved at this high tension; Kate Cookham, her face fixed on him, only waited with a stiff appearance of leaving him, not for dignity but—to an effect of even deeper perversity—for kindness, free to choose. It yet somehow affected him at present, this attitude, as a gage of her *knowing too*—knowing, that is, that he wasn't really free, that this was the thinnest of vain parades, the poorest of hollow heroics, that his need, his solitude, his suffered wrong, his exhausted rancour, his foredoomed submission to any shown interest, all hung together too heavy on him to let the weak wings of his pride do more than vaguely tremble. They couldn't, they didn't carry him a single beat further away; according to which he stood rooted, neither retreating nor advancing, but presently correcting his own share of the bleak exchange by looking off at the sea. Deeply conscious of the awkwardness this posture gave him, he yet clung to it as the last shred of his honour, to the clear argument that it was one thing for him to have felt beneath all others, the previous days, that she was to be counted on, but quite a different for her to have felt that *he* was. His checked approach, arriving thus at no term, could in these odd conditions have established that he wasn't only if Kate Cookham had, as either of them might have said, taken it so—if she had given up the game at last by rising, by walking away and adding to the distance between them, and he had then definitely let her vanish into space. It became a fact that when she did finally rise—though after how long our record scarce takes on itself to say—it was not to confirm their separation but to put an end to it; and this by slowly approaching him till she had come within earshot He had wondered, once aware of it in spite of his averted face, what she would say and on what note, as it were, she would break their week's silence; so that he had to recognise anew, her voice reaching him, that remarkable quality in her which again and again came up for him as her art.

"There are twelve hundred and sixty pounds, to be definite, but I have it all down for you—and you've only to draw."

They lost themselves, these words, rare and exquisite, in the wide bright genial medium and the Sunday stillness, but even while that occurred and he was gaping for it she was herself there, in her battered ladylike truth, to answer for them, to represent them, and, if a further grace than their simple syllabled beauty were conceivable, almost embarrassingly to cause them to materialise. Yes, she let her smart and tight little reticule hang as if it bulged, beneath its clasp, with the whole portentous sum, and he felt himself glare again at this vividest of her attested claims. She might have been ready, on the spot, to open the store to the plunge of his hand, or, with the situation otherwise conceived, to impose on his pauperised state an acceptance of alms on a scale unprecedented in the annals of street charity. Nothing so much counted for him, however, neither grave numeral nor elegant fraction, as the short, rich, rounded word that the breeze had picked up as it dropped and seemed now to blow about between them. "To draw—to draw?" Yes, he gaped it as if it had no sense; the fact being that even while he did so he was reading into her use of the term more romance than any word in the language had ever had for him. He, Herbert Dodd, was to live to "draw," like people, scarce hampered by the conditions of earth, whom he had remotely and circuitously heard about, and in fact when he walked back with her to where she had been sitting it was very much, for his strained nerves, as if the very bench of desolation itself were to be the scene of that exploit and he mightn't really live till he reached it.

When they had sat down together she did press the spring of her reticule, from which she took, not a handful of gold nor a packet of crisp notes, but an oblong sealed letter, which she had thus waited on him, she remarked, on purpose to deliver, and which would certify, with sundry particulars, to the credit she had opened for him at a London bank. He received it without looking at it—he held it, in the same manner, conspicuous and unassimilated, for most of the rest of the immediate time, appearing embarrassed with it, nervously twisting and flapping it, yet thus publicly retaining it even while aware, beneath everything, of the strange, the quite dreadful, wouldn't it be? engagement that such inaction practically stood for. He could accept money to that amount, yes—but not for nothing in return. For what then in return? He kept asking himself for what, while she said other things and made above all, in her high, shrewd, successful way the point that, no, he needn't pretend that his conviction of her continued personal interest in him wouldn't have tided him over any question besetting him since their separation. She put it to him that the deep instinct of where he should at last find her must confidently have worked for him, since she confessed to her instinct of where she should find *him*; which meant—oh it came home to him as he fingered his sealed treasure!—neither more nor less than that she had now created between them an equality of experience. He wasn't to have done all the suffering, *she* was to have "been through" things he couldn't even guess at; and, since he was bargaining away his right ever again to allude to the unforgettable, so much there was of it, what her tacit proposition came to was that they were "square" and might start afresh.

He didn't take up her charge, as his so compromised "pride" yet in a manner prompted him, that he had enjoyed all the week all those elements of ease about her; the most he achieved for that was to declare, with an ingenuity contributing to float him no small distance further, that of course he had turned up at their old place of tryst, which had been, through the years, the haunt of his solitude and the goal of his walk any Sunday morning that seemed too beautiful for church; but that he hadn't in the least built on her presence there—since that supposition gave him, she would understand, wouldn't she? the air, disagreeable to him, of having come in search of her. Her quest of himself, once he had been seated there, would have been another matter—but in short "Of course after all you did come to me, just now, didn't you?" He felt himself, too, lamely and gracelessly grin, as for the final kick of his honour, in confirmation of the record that he had then yielded but to her humility. Her humility became for him at this hour and to this tune, on the bench of desolation, a quantity more prodigious and even more mysterious than that other guaranteed quantity the finger-tips of his left hand could feel the tap by the action of his right; though what was in especial extraordinary was the manner in which she could keep making him such allowances and yet meet him again, at some turn, as with her residuum for her clever self so great.

"Come to you, Herbert Dodd?" she imperturbably echoed.

"I've been coming to you for the last ten years!"

There had been for him just before this sixty supreme seconds of intensest aspiration—a minute of his keeping his certificate poised for a sharp thrust back at her, the thrust of the wild freedom of his saying: "No, no, I *can't* give them up; I can't simply sink them deep down in my soul forever, with no cross in all my future to mark *that* burial; so that if this is what our arrangement means I must decline to have anything to do with it." The words none the less hadn't come, and when she had herself, a couple of minutes later, spoken those others, the blood rose to his face as if, given his stiffness and her extravagance, he had just indeed saved himself.

Everything in fact stopped, even his fidget with his paper; she imposed a hush, she imposed at any rate the conscious decent form of one, and he couldn't afterward have told how long, at this juncture, he must have sat simply gazing before him. It was so long, at any rate, that Kate herself got up—and quite indeed, presently, as if her own forms were now at an end. He had returned her nothing—so what was she waiting for? She had been on the two other occasions momentarily at a loss, but never so much so, no doubt, as was thus testified to by her leaving the bench and moving over once more to the rail of the terrace. She could carry it off, in a manner, with her resources, that she was waiting with so little to wait for; she could face him again, after looking off at the sea, as if this slightly stiff delay, not wholly exempt from awkwardness, had been but a fine scruple of her courtesy. She had gathered herself in; after giving him time to appeal she could take it that he had decided and that nothing was left for her to do. "Well then," she clearly launched at him across the broad walk—"well then, good-bye."

Henry James

She had come nearer with it, as if he might rise for some show of express separation; but he only leaned back motionless, his eyes on her now—he kept her a moment before him. "Do you mean that we don't—that we don't—?" But he broke down.

"Do I 'mean'—?" She remained as for questions he might ask, but it was wellnigh as if there played through her dotty veil an irrepressible irony for that particular one. "I've meant, for long years, I think, all I'm capable of meaning. I've meant so much that I can't mean more. So there it is."

"But if you go," he appealed—and with a sense as of final flatness, however he arranged it, for his own attitude—"but if you go sha'n't I see you again?"

She waited a little, and it was strangely for him now as if—though at last so much more gorged with her tribute than she had ever been with his—something still depended on her. "Do you *like* to see me?" she very simply asked.

At this he did get up; that was easier than to say—at least with responsive simplicity; and again for a little he looked hard and in silence at his letter; which at last, however, raising his eyes to her own for the act, while he masked their conscious ruefulness, to his utmost, in some air of assurance, he slipped into the inner pocket of his coat, letting it settle there securely. "You're too wonderful." But he frowned at her with it as never in his life. "Where does it all come from?"

"The wonder of poor me?" Kate Cookham said. "It comes from *you*."

He shook his head slowly—feeling, with his letter there against his heart, such a new agility, almost such a new range of interest. "I mean so *much* money—so extraordinarily much."

Well, she held him a while blank. "Does it seem to you extraordinarily much—twelve-hundred-and-sixty? Because, you know," she added, "it's all."

"It's enough!" he returned with a slight thoughtful droop of his head to the right and his eyes attached to the far horizon as through a shade of shyness for what he was saying. He felt all her own lingering nearness somehow on his cheek.

"It's enough? Thank you then!" she rather oddly went on.

He shifted a little his posture. "It was more than a hundred a year—for you to get together."

"Yes," she assented, "that was what year by year I tried for."

"But that you could live all the while and save that—!" Yes, he was at liberty, as he hadn't been, quite pleasantly to marvel. All his wonderments in life had been hitherto unanswered—and didn't the change mean that here again was the social relation?

"Ah, I didn't live as you saw me the other day."

"Yes," he answered—and didn't he the next instant feel he must fairly have smiled with it?—"the other day you *were* going it!"

"For once in my life," said Kate Cookham. "I've left the hotel," she after a moment added.

"Ah, you're in—a—lodgings?" he found himself inquiring as for positive sociability.

She had apparently a slight shade of hesitation, but in an instant it was all right; as what he showed he wanted to know she seemed mostly to give him. "Yes—but far of course from here. Up on the hill." To which, after another instant, "At The Mount, Castle Terrace," she subjoined.

"Oh, I *know* The Mount. And Castle Terrace is awfully sunny and nice."

"Awfully sunny and nice," Kate Cookham took from him.

"So that if it isn't," he pursued, "like the Royal, why you're at least comfortable."

"I shall be comfortable anywhere now," she replied with a certain dryness.

It was astonishing, however, what had become of his own. "Because I've accepted—?"

"Call it that!" she dimly smiled.

"I hope then at any rate," he returned, "you can now thoroughly rest" He spoke as for a cheerful conclusion and moved again also to smile, though as with a poor grimace, no doubt; since what he seemed most clearly to feel was that since he "accepted" he mustn't, for his last note, have accepted in sulkiness or gloom. With that, at the same time, he couldn't but know, in all his fibres, that with such a still-watching face as the dotty veil didn't disguise for him there was no possible concluding, at least on his part On hers, on hers it was—as he had so often for a week had reflectively to pronounce things—another affair. Ah, somehow, both formidably and helpfully, her face concluded—yet in a sense so strangely enshrouded in things she didn't tell him. What *must* she, what mustn't she, have done? What she had said—

and she had really told him nothing—was no account of her life; in the midst of which conflict of opposed recognitions, at any rate, it was as if, for all he could do, he himself now considerably floundered. "But I can't think—I can't think—!"

"You can't think I can have made so much money in the time and been honest?"

"Oh, you've been *honest!*" Herbert Dodd distinctly allowed.

It moved her stillness to a gesture—which, however, she had as promptly checked; and she went on the next instant as for further generosity to his failure of thought. "Everything was possible, under my stress, with my hatred."

"Your hatred—?" For she had paused as if it were after all too difficult.

"Of what I should for so long have been doing to you."

With this, for all his failures, a greater light than any yet shone upon him. "It made you think of ways—?"

"It made me think of everything. It made me work," said Kate Cookham. She added, however, the next moment: "But that's my story."

"And I mayn't hear it?"

"No—because I mayn't hear yours."

"Oh, mine—!" he said with the strangest, saddest, yet after all most resigned sense of surrender of it; which he tried to make sound as if he couldn't have told it, for its splendor of sacrifice and of misery, even if he would.

It seemed to move in her a little, exactly, that sense of the invidious. "Ah, mine too, I assure you—!"

He rallied at once to the interest. "Oh, we *can* talk then?"

"Never," she all oddly replied. "Never," said Kate Cookham.

They remained so, face to face; the effect of which for him was that he had after a little understood why. That was fundamental. "Well, I see."

Thus confronted they stayed; and then, as he saw with a contentment that came up from deeper still, it was indeed she who, with her worn fine face, would conclude. "But I can take care of you."

"You *have!*" he said as with nothing left of him but a beautiful appreciative candour.

"Oh, but you'll want it now in a way—!" she responsibly answered.

He waited a moment, dropping again on the seat. So, while she still stood, he looked up at her; with the sense somehow that there were too many things and that they were all together, terribly, irresistibly, doubtless blessedly, in her eyes and her whole person; which thus affected him for the moment as more than he could bear. He leaned forward, dropping his elbows to his knees and pressing his head on his hands. So he stayed, saying nothing; only, with the sense of her own sustained, renewed and wonderful action, knowing that an arm had passed round him and that he was held. She was beside him on the bench of desolation.

ABOUT THE AUTHOR

 **Henry James** OM (April 15, 1843 – February 28, 1916), son of theologian Henry James Sr. and brother of the philosopher and psychologist William James and diarist Alice James, was an American-born author and literary critic of the late 19th and early 20th centuries. He spent much of his life in Europe and became a British subject shortly before his death. He is primarily known for novels, novellas and short stories based on themes of consciousness and morality.

James significantly contributed to the criticism of fiction, particularly in his insistence that writers be allowed the greatest freedom possible in presenting their view of the world. His imaginative use of point of view, interior mono-logue and possibly unreliable narrators in his own novels and tales brought a new depth and interest to narrative fiction. An extraordinarily productive writer, he published substantive books of travel writing, biography, autobio-graphy and visual arts criticism.

In all, he wrote 22 novels, including two left unfinished at his death, and 112 tales of varying lengths, along with many plays and a large number of non-fiction essays and books.

Choose from Thousands of 1stWorldLibrary Classics By

A. M. Barnard
Ada Leverson
Adolphus William Ward
Aesop
Agatha Christie
Alexander Aaronsohn
Alexander Kielland
Alexandre Dumas
Alfred Gatty
Alfred Ollivant
Alice Duer Miller
Alice Turner Curtis
Alice Dunbar
Allen Chapman
Alleyne Ireland
Ambrose Bierce
Amelia E. Barr
Amory H. Bradford
Andrew Lang
Andrew McFarland Davis
Andy Adams
Angela Brazil
Anna Alice Chapin
Anna Sewell
Annie Besant
Annie Hamilton Donnell
Annie Payson Call
Annie Roe Carr
Annonaymous
Anton Chekhov
Archibald Lee Fletcher
Arnold Bennett
Arthur C. Benson
Arthur Conan Doyle
Arthur M. Winfield
Arthur Ransome
Arthur Schnitzler
Arthur Train
Atticus
B.H. Baden-Powell
B. M. Bower
B. C. Chatterjee
Baroness Emmuska Orczy
Baroness Orczy
Basil King
Bayard Taylor
Ben Macomber
Bertha Muzzy Bower
Bjornstjerne Bjornson

Booth Tarkington
Boyd Cable
Bram Stoker
C. Collodi
C. E. Orr
C. M. Ingleby
Carolyn Wells
Catherine Parr Traill
Charles A. Eastman
Charles Amory Beach
Charles Dickens
Charles Dudley Warner
Charles Farrar Browne
Charles Ives
Charles Kingsley
Charles Klein
Charles Hanson Towne
Charles Lathrop Pack
Charles Romyn Dake
Charles Whibley
Charles Willing Beale
Charlotte M. Braeme
Charlotte M. Yonge
Charlotte Perkins Stetson
Clair W. Hayes
Clarence Day Jr.
Clarence E. Mulford
Clemence Housman
Confucius
Coningsby Dawson
Cornelis DeWitt Wilcox
Cyril Burleigh
D. H. Lawrence
Daniel Defoe
David Garnett
Dinah Craik
Don Carlos Janes
Donald Keyhoe
Dorothy Kilner
Dougan Clark
Douglas Fairbanks
E. Nesbit
E. P. Roe
E. Phillips Oppenheim
E. S. Brooks
Earl Barnes
Edgar Rice Burroughs
Edith Van Dyne
Edith Wharton

Edward Everett Hale
Edward J. O'Biren
Edward S. Ellis
Edwin L. Arnold
Eleanor Atkins
Eleanor Hallowell Abbott
Eliot Gregory
Elizabeth Gaskell
Elizabeth McCracken
Elizabeth Von Arnim
Ellem Key
Emerson Hough
Emilie F. Carlen
Emily Bronte
Emily Dickinson
Enid Bagnold
Enilor Macartney Lane
Erasmus W. Jones
Ernie Howard Pie
Ethel May Dell
Ethel Turner
Ethel Watts Mumford
Eugene Sue
Eugenie Foa
Eugene Wood
Eustace Hale Ball
Evelyn Everett-green
Everard Cotes
F. H. Cheley
F. J. Cross
F. Marion Crawford
Fannie E. Newberry
Federick Austin Ogg
Ferdinand Ossendowski
Fergus Hume
Florence A. Kilpatrick
Fremont B. Deering
Francis Bacon
Francis Darwin
Frances Hodgson Burnett
Frances Parkinson Keyes
Frank Gee Patchin
Frank Harris
Frank Jewett Mather
Frank L. Packard
Frank V. Webster
Frederic Stewart Isham
Frederick Trevor Hill
Frederick Winslow Taylor

Friedrich Kerst
Friedrich Nietzsche
Fyodor Dostoyevsky
G.A. Henty
G.K. Chesterton
Gabrielle E. Jackson
Garrett P. Serviss
Gaston Leroux
George A. Warren
George Ade
Geroge Bernard Shaw
George Cary Eggleston
George Durston
George Ebers
George Eliot
George Gissing
George MacDonald
George Meredith
George Orwell
George Sylvester Viereck
George Tucker
George W. Cable
George Wharton James
Gertrude Atherton
Gordon Casserly
Grace E. King
Grace Gallatin
Grace Greenwood
Grant Allen
Guillermo A. Sherwell
Gulielma Zollinger
Gustav Flaubert
H. A. Cody
H. B. Irving
H.C. Bailey
H. G. Wells
H. H. Munro
H. Irving Hancock
H. R. Naylor
H. Rider Haggard
H. W. C. Davis
Haldeman Julius
Hall Caine
Hamilton Wright Mabie
Hans Christian Andersen
Harold Avery
Harold McGrath
Harriet Beecher Stowe
Harry Castlemon
Harry Coghill
Harry Houidini

Hayden Carruth
Helent Hunt Jackson
Helen Nicolay
Hendrik Conscience
Hendy David Thoreau
Henri Barbusse
Henrik Ibsen
Henry Adams
Henry Ford
Henry Frost
Henry James
Henry Jones Ford
Henry Seton Merriman
Henry W Longfellow
Herbert A. Giles
Herbert Carter
Herbert N. Casson
Herman Hesse
Hildegard G. Frey
Homer
Honore De Balzac
Horace B. Day
Horace Walpole
Horatio Alger Jr.
Howard Pyle
Howard R. Garis
Hugh Lofting
Hugh Walpole
Humphry Ward
Ian Maclaren
Inez Haynes Gillmore
Irving Bacheller
Isabel Cecilia Williams
Isabel Hornibrook
Israel Abrahams
Ivan Turgenev
J.G.Austin
J. Henri Fabre
J. M. Barrie
J. M. Walsh
J. Macdonald Oxley
J. R. Miller
J. S. Fletcher
J. S. Knowles
J. Storer Clouston
J. W. Duffield
Jack London
Jacob Abbott
James Allen
James Andrews
James Baldwin

James Branch Cabell
James DeMille
James Joyce
James Lane Allen
James Lane Allen
James Oliver Curwood
James Oppenheim
James Otis
James R. Driscoll
Jane Abbott
Jane Austen
Jane L. Stewart
Janet Aldridge
Jens Peter Jacobsen
Jerome K. Jerome
Jessie Graham Flower
John Buchan
John Burroughs
John Cournos
John F. Kennedy
John Gay
John Glasworthy
John Habberton
John Joy Bell
John Kendrick Bangs
John Milton
John Philip Sousa
John Taintor Foote
Jonas Lauritz Idemil Lie
Jonathan Swift
Joseph A. Altsheler
Joseph Carey
Joseph Conrad
Joseph E. Badger Jr
Joseph Hergesheimer
Joseph Jacobs
Jules Vernes
Julian Hawthrone
Julie A Lippmann
Justin Huntly McCarthy
Kakuzo Okakura
Karle Wilson Baker
Kate Chopin
Kenneth Grahame
Kenneth McGaffey
Kate Langley Bosher
Kate Langley Bosher
Katherine Cecil Thurston
Katherine Stokes
L. A. Abbot
L. T. Meade

L. Frank Baum
Latta Griswold
Laura Dent Crane
Laura Lee Hope
Laurence Housman
Lawrence Beasley
Leo Tolstoy
Leonid Andreyev
Lewis Carroll
Lewis Sperry Chafer
Lilian Bell
Lloyd Osbourne
Louis Hughes
Louis Joseph Vance
Louis Tracy
Louisa May Alcott
Lucy Fitch Perkins
Lucy Maud Montgomery
Luther Benson
Lydia Miller Middleton
Lyndon Orr
M. Corvus
M. H. Adams
Margaret E. Sangster
Margret Howth
Margaret Vandercook
Margaret W. Hungerford
Margret Penrose
Maria Edgeworth
Maria Thompson Daviess
Mariano Azuela
Marion Polk Angellotti
Mark Overton
Mark Twain
Mary Austin
Mary Catherine Crowley
Mary Cole
Mary Hastings Bradley
Mary Roberts Rinehart
Mary Rowlandson
M. Wollstonecraft Shelley
Maud Lindsay
Max Beerbohm
Myra Kelly
Nathaniel Hawthrone
Nicolo Machiavelli
O. F. Walton
Oscar Wilde

Owen Johnson
P.G. Wodehouse
Paul and Mabel Thorne
Paul G. Tomlinson
Paul Severing
Percy Brebner
Percy Keese Fitzhugh
Peter B. Kyne
Plato
Quincy Allen
R. Derby Holmes
R. L. Stevenson
R. S. Ball
Rabindranath Tagore
Rahul Alvares
Ralph Bonehill
Ralph Henry Barbour
Ralph Victor
Ralph Waldo Emmerson
Rene Descartes
Ray Cummings
Rex Beach
Rex E. Beach
Richard Harding Davis
Richard Jefferies
Richard Le Gallienne
Robert Barr
Robert Frost
Robert Gordon Anderson
Robert L. Drake
Robert Lansing
Robert Lynd
Robert Michael Ballantyne
Robert W. Chambers
Rosa Nouchette Carey
Rudyard Kipling
Saint Augustine
Samuel B. Allison
Samuel Hopkins Adams
Sarah Bernhardt
Sarah C. Hallowell
Selma Lagerlof
Sherwood Anderson
Sigmund Freud
Standish O'Grady
Stanley Weyman
Stella Benson
Stella M. Francis

Stephen Crane
Stewart Edward White
Stijn Streuvels
Swami Abhedananda
Swami Parmananda
T. S. Ackland
T. S. Arthur
The Princess Der Ling
Thomas A. Janvier
Thomas A Kempis
Thomas Anderton
Thomas Bailey Aldrich
Thomas Bulfinch
Thomas De Quincey
Thomas Dixon
Thomas H. Huxley
Thomas Hardy
Thomas More
Thornton W. Burgess
U. S. Grant
Upton Sinclair
Valentine Williams
Various Authors
Vaughan Kester
Victor Appleton
Victor G. Durham
Victoria Cross
Virginia Woolf
Wadsworth Camp
Walter Camp
Walter Scott
Washington Irving
Wilbur Lawton
Wilkie Collins
Willa Cather
Willard F. Baker
William Dean Howells
William le Queux
W. Makepeace Thackeray
William W. Walter
William Shakespeare
Winston Churchill
Yei Theodora Ozaki
Yogi Ramacharaka
Young E. Allison
Zane Grey